WO**M**EN

BREAKING THROUGH

To my parents
Ed and Peg Swiss

Visit Peterson's on the Internet at http://www.petersons.com

Women Breaking Through is published by Peterson's/Pacesetter Books.

Pacesetter Books, Peterson's/Pacesetter Books, and the Pacesetter horse design are registered trademarks of Peterson's, A Division of Thomson Information Inc.

Library of Congress Cataloging-in-Publication Data

Swiss, Deborah J.
    Women breaking through : overcoming the final 10 obstacles at work / Deborah J. Swiss.
      p.   cm.
    Includes index.
    ISBN 1-56079-535-2
    1. Women—Employment. 2. Women—Promotions. 3. Success in business. I. Title.
HD6053.S89   1996
650.1'082—dc20   96-12919
                                              CIP

Editorial direction by Carol Hupping
Production supervision by Bernadette Boylan
Copyediting by Kathleen Salazar
Proofreading by Joanne Schauffele

Composition by Gary Rozmierski
Creative direction by Linda Huber
Interior design by Cynthia Boone

Printed in the United States of America

10 9 8 7 6 5 4 3 2 1

CONTENTS

ACKNOWLEDGMENTS

I am very lucky to have many friends who offered encouragement and humor throughout this project: Anne Blodget, Laura Boyer, Kay Coughlin, Marvin Green, Cynthia Johnson, Kathy Puccia, Bija Satterlee, and Judy and Harry Warren. Audrey Block and Judy Walker provided extraordinary support, helpful advice, and cheerful voice mail messages through every stage of the writing process.

It was a pleasure to work with Carol Hupping—a superb editor whose excellent judgment and unwavering support made this a much better book. High praise also goes to Kathy Salazar, who gracefully moved mountains in the final production stages. Many thanks to Mike Snell, my agent, mentor, and good friend. I appreciate the first-rate transcription skills provided by Cherie Potts and Pat Steffens. And I thank all of the women I interviewed for their time and their inspiration.

A special thank you to my daughter Alison whose enthusiastic support played a major role in completing this project. With love and admiration, I dedicate this book to my parents.

INTRODUCTION

THE NEW AGENDA

While viewing the national news one evening, I watched with great interest the coverage of a rescue by a television news crew. A young boy had fallen off a bridge close to where a news crew was filming another story. I saw a female reporter in a bright red dress swim quickly to the place where the boy had fallen in the water. Once she reached the boy, a male crew member started yelling commands: "Be careful! Hold onto him! Don't let go!" Slowly and methodically, the woman brought the young boy close to shore where the male crew member took over and carried the boy to dry ground. Soon, the man, huffing and puffing, was interviewed for what had become *his* heroic rescue. And in the background, I noticed the sopping wet woman reporter in the red dress, quietly catching her breath while heading toward the news van.

Struck by how powerfully gender permeates the daily events in which we participate, I recognized the high symbolism attached to this brief incident: the lens through which we judge these activities, the way we view our own accomplishments, and the signals we send our daughters and sons who witness these events.

Nowhere are our perceptions about gender more important than where most of us spend the majority of our waking hours: in the workplace. But why are we, in 1996, still talking about gender issues at work?

Because despite the media hype, the CEO breakfast meetings, the women's conferences, and the progressive policies on paper, equal treatment and opportunity on the job remains a distant goal for too many women. Sometime in the last decade, the progress of women at work came to a quick halt, with too many business leaders saying one thing but practicing another.

1

I began this book with the intention of showcasing organizations that have made a concerted effort to clear the traditional career roadblocks faced by women at work. But the thoughtful responses I received from the remarkable women who took the time to complete my detailed, five-page survey; the information that surfaced in the interviews I conducted later with many of them; and the articles, videotapes, and publications that they sent me from their professional associations tell a different story than the one I had at first hoped to relate. (A summary of survey results can be found on page 219.)

My national cross section of 325 women represents nearly every career field: finance, law, telecommunications, banking, insurance, consulting, marketing, real estate, general management, manufacturing, medicine, engineering, and science. One quarter of the women occupy senior management positions. The rest are in middle or upper-middle management. Their stories revealed disturbing information about the persistent gap between most of their organizations' espoused equal opportunity policies and their actual impact on women's work lives.

Only 17 percent of the women I surveyed report that gender bias does not exist in their place of work. The size of the organization makes little difference in whether or not a woman experiences gender bias or whether she perceives barriers to her career, with the exception of women who run their own businesses. Forty-two percent work in large organizations with more than 3,000 employees; 19 percent are in companies with 501 to 3,000; 21 percent in organizations with 101 to 500; and 18 percent in small firms or companies with under 100 employees.

The majority of the women are at the peak of their careers—in the 35-to-49 age group. Sixty-five percent are married; 60 percent are mothers. Among the women, 29 percent hold M.B.A.'s and 20 percent hold an M.A. or M.S., while 18 percent have J.D.'s, 6 percent have Ph.D.'s, and 3 percent have M.D.'s.

These women are clearly successful in their professions. But despite the degree of success each has achieved, the overwhelming majority agree on gender inequity's unshakable persistence. Even among stellar performers, differential and exclusionary treatment challenges their careers on many fronts: pace of advancement, performance standards, compensation, opportunity to take professional risks, access to business relationship-building, support from top management.

That is the bad news.

But there is also good news. Offering a preview of what I predict will become a critical turning point in the history of women at work, the themes that emerged from forty in-depth personal interviews and more than 1,200 pages of interview transcripts reveal a new momentum among women to ensure themselves equal opportunity and career advancement.

Women Breaking Through is these women's stories—about how they are taking action to end once and for all the often unconscious, but at times deliberate behind-the-scenes rules of work that sabotage so many women's productivity and recognition. And it is a book of strategies for overhauling these unspoken rules at every level of the workplace.

It is not about male-bashing, nor is it about women whining. Rather, it is an examination of generally accepted but nonetheless ill-founded assumptions about ability, teamwork, professional visibility, channels for workplace communication, management style, and work/life choices—and effective ways to turn around attitudes responsible for such assumptions.

Women Breaking Through is designed to answer the following questions, key to creating a work environment with no inherent barriers for women:

- Why do so many thousands of talented women find their professional ability and personal ambition unnecessarily challenged by a silent wall of workplace exclusion?

- Which strategies are effective in overhauling the unwritten rules that sustain an unsupportive work environment and stifle women's careers?

- What can women do to function as members of "the team" while changing the rules?

The research Judy Walker and I conducted for *Women and the Work/Family Dilemma* four years ago identified the "maternal wall" and the huge gap between "family-friendly" policies on paper and their actual support in daily management practice. My research for this book revealed a similar corporate failing in addressing equal opportunity for women at work.

Business leaders have been able to look the other way when it comes to real equality, but that is becoming increasingly difficult for them to do because women are starting to set the agenda for change. Their confidence and clarity of vision about what needs to be done and their pragmatic strategies for doing it are encouraging and helping other women at all levels in all organizations to overcome the remaining obstacles they face.

It is my hope that their stories—at times triumphant, at times heart wrenching—will inspire women to open all of the doors for equal opportunity.

CHAPTER 1

TAKING STOCK

"Women hold up half the sky."

—Ancient Chinese proverb

When I sent surveys to a national cross section of working women—325 in all—I had hoped to identify creative and cost-effective initiatives from organizations truly committed to recruiting and retaining the best and the brightest: women and men. Instead, with a small number of exceptions, the women told me that their organizations remain stuck in some bad habits, and it doesn't look as if things are going to change on their own any time soon.

Like quicksand, deeply entrenched organizational attitudes have stopped gender reform in its tracks. But what I also discovered in my survey and interviews was that there are many women, in workplaces as diverse as Wall Street, the Goddard Space Flight Center, First Boston Corporation, and the automotive industry, who are making change happen. Rather than blaming the system, these women are figuring out how to fix it themselves.

Their scripts for success read unemotionally and without malice toward men. Deflecting self-blame and putting aside defensiveness, they look on gender bias this way: It's real. It can damage my career. So what am I going to do to ensure my own equal opportunity? And what can I do to help other women in the next office?

Amidst the noisy debate about affirmative action and reverse discrimination and the bitter disagreement over who should bear responsibility for which social injustices, these women are, without fanfare, creating new models to achieve workplace equality. They have no interest whatsoever in special treatment or tokenism. Their goal is clear: fair access to information and people critical to career success and the opportunity to advance according to their talent, potential, and hard work.

The Truth About Gender Bias

When Sandra Bartlett* was hired for her first job at an insurance company in 1961, women were required to sign in every morning—in red if they were late—and men were not. Given the fact that the newspaper ran separate ads for male and female candidates, Sandra considered herself lucky to have landed a job as an underwriter. These were the days when interviewers without hesitation and without legal repercussions would tell her, "I'm sorry—you passed all the aptitude tests, but we're going to hire a man instead of you because women have babies."

Many of the senior managers I met told me that the rules of work were clearer back then, when bias was openly sanctioned in their organizations. Today's more subtle discrimination can make it more difficult to identify and thus to remedy. As one engineer suggests, "For the most part, gender discrimination is not overt. You come to realize it's there, lurking behind the doors of the men's room, when you overhear comments made between men in the office."

Like Sandra, many women have, in the past, silently watched the gender-tracking that often begins as soon as they walk into their first job. As the years go by, they wait in frustration for the CEO's equal opportunity message to filter down to line management. But it seldom does. Those who hold the most direct power to change

---

* Most of the names in this book are real, but some of the women I interviewed requested a pseudonym. Its use is indicated with an asterisk.

workplace standards are either so comfortable with them that they truly do not see their exclusionary effect on women, or they simply find the prospect of change too difficult or too threatening. The threat, and even the reality, of litigation for discrimination and sexual harassment has done little to change accepted corporate behavior. It has only pushed it underground a bit.

Why don't women themselves just speak up? The answer has everything to do with economic survival. Most successful women realistically cannot make waves and risk career jeopardy. They have already faced enough turbulence in their daily work lives. As one bank president observed, "Women learn not to complain because it's considered whining and it can only hurt our careers. But we live with a lot of frustration."

THE FACTS ABOUT WOMEN AT WORK

- **The salary gap mirrors the gender gap.**
  Sixty-eight percent of the women I surveyed believe that being a woman has limited their opportunity for fair compensation. Women at the top of their organizations felt this just as strongly as those in middle and upper-middle management. A disturbing 40 percent do not believe they are paid at the same level as male colleagues with the same credentials.

  Women today earn, on average, 28 percent less than the men sitting at the desks next to them. More troubling is evidence that pay disparity for women rises along with promotions and career development. In 1993, the *Wall Street Journal* reported that "female financial managers—including those who close multimillion deals—earned only 62 cents on the male dollar."[1] Female securities brokers fared worse at 52 cents on that dollar.[2]

  The wage gap widens as a woman grows older. Among workers ages 25–29, women earn 86 percent of the take-home pay of their male counterparts; by ages 55–59, women earn only 59 percent of male earnings.[3]

- **Moving women into the managerial pipeline has done little to advance deserving ones into senior management.**

  Sixty-seven percent of the women in my survey believe that gender has limited their options for promotions. A human resources manager for a financial-services firm raised the question many women would like to ask their CEOs: "You have actively recruited women for many years—50 percent at the entry professional level—but less than 5 percent make it to the top. It's no longer a pipeline issue. What changes will you make to correct this situation?"

  Despite twenty solid years in management, women hold fewer than one third of the managerial jobs within the 38,000 companies that file Equal Employment Opportunity Commission (EEOC) reports.[4] Women account for only 6.9 percent of the 11,700 corporate board directors.[5]

  A 1993 survey of 1,233 women and 710 men in advertising, broadcasting, and publishing revealed a vivid contrast in perceptions about gender bias. While the male respondents indicated that they believe women have equal opportunities for pay, promotion, and advancement, quantitative survey results disputed this assertion. Among women and men with less than five years of experience, men were paid, on average, $6,700 per year more; at five to nine years on the job, the salary gap widened to $12,600; for those with ten to nineteen years in the field, men earned, on average, $21,700 more than their female counterparts each year.[6]

- **Gender, not talent, is often the deciding factor in who is offered committee leadership or the golden client.**

  Nearly 60 percent of the women I surveyed in middle and upper-middle management believe that being a woman has limited opportunities to take on high-visibility assignments in their organizations. This perception is undoubtedly linked to realities about the informal mentoring that heightens potential for the high-risk/high-reward assignment. Almost the same number of the women believe that gender has limited their opportunities to have a mentor.

■ **Progressive policies on paper are meaningless in the absence of support from top management and line supervisors.**

Despite the fact that 73 percent of the women in my survey reported that their organizations have taken some action to promote gender equity, 62 percent have been faced with gender bias in their current positions. Sixty-nine percent have experienced language demeaning to women in their current jobs.

A national study by the Families and Work Institute revealed that 39 percent of the women managers rated their opportunities for advancement as "poor" or "fair" compared with 16 percent of their male counterparts.[7]

■ **An absence of objective performance standards against which everyone is judged perpetuates the double standard.**

Sixty-eight percent of the women in my sample believe they are held to a higher performance standard than their male colleagues. This belief is fortified not by random and capricious observations but by comparing their cumulative career experiences with the men with whom they trained in college, business school, and law school. A 1995 *Fortune* magazine survey of 300 women managers and executives echoed these findings.[8]

■ **Sexual harassment continues to be a silent partner in maintaining an unsupportive work environment for women.**

Half of the women in my survey have experienced sexual harassment on the job, defined as "unwelcome sexual advances, requests for sexual favors, and other verbal or physical conduct of a sexual nature." Most have been harassed more than once, with superiors named most often as the offender. Eighty-five percent handled the incident privately with the offending individual. Many revealed that they had never before disclosed to anyone the harassment, which they found embarrassing and demoralizing.

■ **Gender bias, not parenting responsibilities, is the factor most likely to slow a woman's advancement.**

Being a parent has little impact on whether a woman faces career obstacles or experiences gender bias on the job. When asked, "Do you foresee any barriers to reaching your career goals?" only a slightly higher percentage of parents answered "Yes" than did the women without children.

Stereotypes about working mothers are, however, viewed as a significant barrier to career success. The majority of respondents believe that once a woman has a child, she is automatically perceived as being less committed to her career. A 1994 *Working Woman* poll of 500 executive women revealed that "the stock explanation of female flight—that most women resign to tend to their families—is overstated."[9]

Another myth attached to a woman's life choices is her unwillingness to relocate. But only 14 percent of the women I surveyed believe that being a woman has significantly limited their ability to take jobs that require a move.

The Pace of Progress

Women have waited—perhaps too patiently—for the old boys' network to retire and for the gender equity problem to dissolve through a gradual social change. Excuses for the pace of progress no longer appease women, who see themselves losing out on opportunities and recognition. They see the faulty logic in the two leading theories about what it will take to achieve gender equity in the workplace:

1. The pipeline theory—the proposition that once the numbers of women have reached a critical mass in the office, gender equity will, through a natural evolution, take hold and that gender equity just needs more time.
2. The work-family myth—the theory that corporate support for work-life balance will proceed to resolve the inequitable treatment of women at work.

The pipeline theory, persistent as a seemingly legitimate excuse for allowing evolution to assume the burden of change, has lost its credibility. Twenty-five years ago, the reasonable response to "Why haven't more women reached equal status in the workplace?" was "There just aren't enough women in the pipeline. You need to wait." Women have done all the right things professionally and waited patiently for the expected results. Instead, as one woman was told by her uncle, an executive in a Fortune 1000 company, "Let's face it. It's still a man's world."

Only two women hold the position of CEO in Fortune 1000 companies.[10] And more women than men are filtered out from consideration for jobs past middle management.[11]

Hard work, exceptional talent, and driving ambition are not enough. The logic behind the pipeline theory—the notion that sheer numbers will make it impossible for gender to limit career potential—has made minimal impact on the overall presence of women in leadership positions. "Just let me prove to you that I can produce outstanding work" can easily lead to the more disturbing reality: "I need to work twice as hard and be twice as good just to stay even with men with the same credentials."

Work-family policies have not led to more opportunities and advancement for women. Companies consistently ranked among the most "family friendly" have done little to shatter the glass ceiling. The DuPont Corporation, an early leader in progressive work-life balance programs, still confronts the reality of showing one of the smallest percentages of female managers (4.5 percent) among its competitors. The *Wall Street Journal* identified the barrier to heightened career progress for women at DuPont: "DuPont's family-friendly policies clearly haven't made huge inroads into management or changing the culture. And many female DuPont employees believe that while Chairman Edgar Woolard Jr. is firmly committed to diversity, there is a whole level of managers beneath him who aren't comfortable working with women."[12]

THE UNWRITTEN RULES OF WORK

Gender inequity—as perpetuated by the unwritten rules of work—is rarely clear-cut. It can be difficult to prove, to quantify, and thus to remedy. As chemist Cynthia Friend observes, "The subtle aspects of how work is judged are the most difficult to overcome. Senior colleagues—all men—tend to want to 'reproduce' by hiring younger people in their own likeness. This leads to inadvertent bias." A Dallas management consultant advises her younger colleagues, "Pay close attention to the unwritten rules—to the real treatment of women. Many men and companies know how to say the right things, but the informal network functions quite differently."

These subtle, yet deeply entrenched, exclusionary traditions are not necessarily the result of poor intentions from senior management. As Sarah Curran*, a vice president at a large manufacturing firm, observes, "Male managers think they are unbiased, which is often worse. This plays itself out in subtle behavior, in differences in the expectations they hold for women and men." More often than not, today's outdated organizational rituals stem from benign neglect of a workforce that bears little resemblance to its founding principals.

What are these rituals, these unspoken "rules" that are destined to favor a man's career and protect the silent wall of exclusion for women? They are as follows:

- Most business leadership derives from a command-and-control style. Women who see the value in collaboration, sharing credit, and team-building are often viewed as lacking the power to lead departments or organizations. Questioning the status quo and proposing a different model for corporate leadership stifles a woman's career.

- The concepts of bottom-up management and real teamwork remain distant goals in most organizations. The real story is that it's still every person for himself or herself. Individual performance is what is recognized and rewarded.

- Those who are groomed and mentored at the bottom and the middle of the organization are often mirror images—in style and gender—of those at the top.

- When in doubt, the safe choice prevails. Whether the issue is a promotion or an assignment to a key project, most managers find it easier to choose someone cast in their own mold.

- Business's second shift—male-only, after-hours socializing and client entertainment—maintains the male advantage during the daytime shift.

- Perceiving is believing. A man and woman using the same words or the same style are evaluated by different sets of standards and expectations.

- "Face time," not productivity, remains a premiere measure of performance in most offices. Relinquishing your soul is a show of real commitment.

TODAY'S AGENDA

The roots of gender inequity are powerful, deep, and prickly. The "men and women are just different" explanation for gender-tracking in the office is too easy an excuse for a woman's often second-class status. Accommodation and assimilation are not the answers, particularly when only women are expected to do most all of the compromising. In an ideal world, different perspectives are heard and recognized, yielding the richness a balanced outlook brings.

What hasn't worked to bring about real and lasting change for women in the workplace? Acceptance by women—"This is awful, but I'm just going to have to live with it"—sustains the status quo and perpetuates an unhealthy and demoralizing attitude of women as victims. Toleration is a poor substitute for improvement.

Playing at being "just like the guys" or being "the good girl" who never complains is heavy baggage to carry along a career track. Stridency, while it can make us feel better in a moment of frustration, defeats our goal of establishing our credibility and acceptance as equal. No matter how good you are, when your defenses are up, your business currency falls in value.

Entitlements weaken a cause when they default into tokenism. Promoting a woman solely on the basis of gender harms the goal of equal opportunity based on merit. Women are not looking for special treatment because of their gender. Tokenism benefits no one and denigrates the talents of the vast majority of deserving women.

Not every male executive is a Neanderthal. Not every woman deserves a promotion before the man down the hall. But with a complete generation of women in the managerial pipeline, it is time to take stock of why it is still necessary to discuss gender equity in the workplace at all.

The women I have gotten to know are remarkable for the strides they have made for themselves and for other women in their organizations. Their stories and strategies, which fill so many pages of this book, center on action in ten key areas:

1. Male/female business relationships: To circumvent the career-limiting influence of the old boys' network, trailblazing women have located new points of access to collegial and client trust. They are beginning to shatter the sanctum of the locker room—the business that takes place after a golf game or over a glass of beer—and are replacing time-honored traditions with new ways to build productive relationships with colleagues and clients.

2. Risk-taking: Comfort with risk is viewed as a necessary and effective component to career development. By taking chances and stepping forward with a compelling style and vision, women are asserting more control over where their careers are headed.

3. The double standard: To address the void in objective compensation and performance standards, women have figured out how to do their own career benchmarking and how to present incontrovertible evidence to rectify bias in pay and promotion systems.

4. The middle-management wall: With a clear confidence in their ability to succeed, women are accelerating their career advancement through tackling and solving complicated business problems and through an unshakable vision for results.

5. Visibility: At first, many women find it difficult to promote themselves on the job. But increasing numbers of women managers are making themselves heard in meetings and are being recognized in their organizations as they amass the sorts of track records that make it impossible for anyone to deny them leadership opportunities.

6. Harassment: Sexual harassment is the barrier to equal opportunity most out of a woman's control. Although the women I surveyed cannot prevent harassment on the job, they have learned how to stop it on their own.

7. Work-life balance: Deeply entrenched attitudes about a single-minded corporate work ethic perpetuate the gap between progressive policies in glossy corporate brochures and the harsh reality of management practice. Progressive women have figured out how to use these policies without derailing their careers.

8. Solidarity among women: The queen bee is dead. Women are joining together and asserting their influence as agents of organizational change. Women across the country—from Pacific Bell to Wall Street to Boston hospitals—are extending a helping hand to one another.

9. Alliance-building: Women are using their well-honed management skills to build alliances with people who will alert them to political land mines, act as confidential sounding boards, and help position their careers for the next important job move.

10. Organizational support: By communicating directly with senior management, by demonstrating the value of new models for work teams and workplace alliances, and by assessing what adds value to their organizations, women are behaving as though they have already won. Their overriding strategy is to find the time and the courage to be an educator for their organizations.

While there is no singular, prepackaged, quick-fix strategy to remedy every permutation of gender bias, the women featured in this book have taken control of their own careers. In so doing, they are beginning to move their organizations across the frontier to a new corporate world where everyone wins.

CHAPTER 2

RESTRUCTURING THE MALE/FEMALE BUSINESS RELATIONSHIP

"What I want—the end goal—is to be treated like an equal. That's what's most important."

—Catherine Lee, law firm partner

Not every man deliberately sets out to misunderstand, exclude, and miscommunicate with his female colleagues. Not every woman's behavior is beyond reproach in how she deals with the men in her office. But at this moment in business and social history, the most common patterns of business behavior are much more likely to exclude a woman than a man.

A whole host of accepted ways of conducting business, based on a male-directed culture, causes some talented women to question: "Do I really belong here?" Others may react with anger at their automatic relegation to outsider status, either seething in silence or leaving their traditional organizations in favor of smaller start-up ventures where the work culture is more inclusive. The conventional workplace rules, reinforced by long-accepted social norms, readily allow a stubborn "good old boy" mentality, often unrecognized and second nature to many executives, to quietly exclude women's full workplace participation.

Ninety-two percent of the women I surveyed view the attitudes of their male colleagues as an obstacle to equal opportunity. Ninety-three percent identified a difference in male/female communication styles as a barrier to equal treatment in a business setting. Seventy-seven percent view the exclusion of women from after-hours socializing as a barrier to professional advancement.

Subtle gender injustices, as corrosive as blatant discrimination, can at first be more difficult to identify, to measure, and to remedy. Sarah Curran*, a vice president at a large manufacturing firm, has witnessed again and again the lack of recognition of women on male-dominated teams: "The classic example is a group of people sitting around a conference table. A woman suggests a new approach. It immediately gets lost in the conversation. Then two minutes later, a man makes the same suggestion and it's 'Wow! What a great idea!' And you sit there and think, 'What just happened?'"

When Sarah has found herself in such a situation, she has, more than once, wanted to blurt out the simple truth: "That's what I suggested a minute ago." Frustratingly, she knows this accurate statement will be perceived as sour grapes or whining. Sarah instead has experimented with a variety of less threatening techniques to make her voice as an outsider heard to "inside" conversations.

For many women, their initial reaction to this lack of recognition is understandably: This is unfair. Why should a woman even need to be concerned about whether her words or behavior threaten her male colleagues? Why should she make the effort to meet her male colleagues more than halfway when some barely recognize her presence in the office?

The answer is that when those with insider status see no need to change, there is no other choice. For the most part, only women—not the men, not the organization—see merit in gender reform. Dismantling the attitudinal walls that have fortified barriers to fully productive male/female business relationships relies on women coming forward. Few men will take the initiative: Some genuinely do not recognize how the male norms for business behavior are excluding women; others simply find it too threatening to change what is perfectly acceptable to them.

In lieu of suffering in silence, the most successful business women I met take a long-term view by choosing strategies that enable their career to survive while promoting new standards for relationship building. Mindful of the real business need to gain support and recognition from their male colleagues, they are, one by one, restructuring the male/female business relationship. In doing so, they are providing us all with answers to these important questions about building gender-fair business teams:

- Is it possible to avoid a defensive posture—from either men or women—while asserting a new model for communication and collaboration between the two?

- How can women ensure that they will be heard and recognized in meetings, accepted and included in informal conversations, and taken seriously at every level of their profession?

- Can a woman who's perceived as an "outsider" because of her gender achieve inside credibility without assuming traditional "male" insider roles and values?

Most successful business transactions demand effective relationship-building, yet many men remain fundamentally uncomfortable with the woman in the next office, in the first instance because of style differences and, more recently, compounded by either fear or misunderstanding about discrimination and sexual harassment issues. This discomfort derives perhaps from the threat of new competition at work or from fear of the unknown. And this discomfort can be further fueled by different approaches to professional style, to teams and sharing credit, to developing client trust, and to business socializing.

Equal treatment for women at work really boils down to realizing the great value of real collaboration between women and men who work side by side. On one level, the issue is so simple. Yet the process can be so difficult.

Finding Common Ground

In shifting her own attitude about entry to conversations traditionally closed to women, Sarah Curran has discovered new opportunities for the kind of relationship-building that takes place in the hallway, the coffee room, and the parking lot. When she sees two men chatting in an elevator, she thinks to herself: "Information is being exchanged. If I were to allow my insecure side to have its way, I'd assume that it's a private conversation and maybe I should take a separate elevator. But I push the confident side of me forward and say to myself: 'I'm just going to jump right into this conversation—and maybe learn, or contribute, something helpful for my work.'" Such action has paid off for Sarah, and she advises women colleagues to do the same. We have to remember, she explains, that many men have *only* worked with other men in managerial positions and will seldom stop to think to invite women into such chats.

Sarah has also found that a private, one-on-one conversation after a meeting is a good opportunity to speak with a senior manager on a sensitive gender issue. It is now second nature for her to ask a man with whom she has already established some credibility: "If you look back on that session, did you notice how the men seemed to listen politely to Jane but never picked up on her ideas? But when John later raised a nearly identical point, the concept suddenly had business validity." Once Sarah has established such a connection with a manager, she's found that she can pass private looks to the man at future meetings. His "Aha! I get it!" reaction is a hopeful sign that he'll listen more carefully to the next woman who speaks in the meeting.

Sarah tries to understand why some men are reluctant to engage in private conversation with a female associate. "They don't want it to look like it's a man and a woman kibitzing about having a drink after work," she says. "Physical surroundings are important to them and should be to women, too. Such talk has to take place in appropriate and unthreatening places."

Oftentimes it takes more than one woman's actions to make even a dent in the codes of conduct that prohibit comfortable relationship-building between men and women. Ellen James*, the only female boss for 250 assembly-line workers, had to gently rebuff a well-intentioned male colleague who wanted to help her establish credibility with her employees. "Hey, Ellen," he said early one morning. "I want to help you because you're very good and you're very smart, and I like working with you. Being a woman manager automatically hurts you in this place because you're the only one. And the fact that you won't yell and swear at people makes you look weak."

Her colleague offered his help in strengthening Ellen's business image: "Why don't we stage a mock fight on the plant floor. We'll yell at one another the way all the men do, but I'll let you win the argument." While Ellen appreciated support from this man, she had no ready response to his "image-building" advice. Her business-school training had never addressed gender as a manager's liability nor had it suggested yelling as a leadership strategy. Ellen now recalls her most enjoyable year at this company as the time she spent on a joint venture with the Japanese: "Nobody screamed to make their point, but what had to be done was well understood. I really enjoyed such a rational work environment."

BREAKING THE VISIBILITY BARRIER

Emily Powers*, a New England attorney, describes the daily references to her outsider status—a status she seems to have acquired purely because of gender. At a recent meeting on a bank merger, Emily was sitting around a table with twelve other people. As is often the case, Emily was the only woman present. "I hadn't noticed I was the only woman because I'm so used to it." After discussing how community groups might react to the merger and the fact that there would be no women on the bank's board, the senior lawyer piped up with: "Hey, why don't you put Emily on your board? She's a woman."

Ironically, Emily was *too* visible as a woman. She viewed her presence in the room differently. "I'm a LAWYER here," she said. "I'm not here to represent all women." Like Emily, many women reported that their presence in a roomful of men often raises one red flag or another: tokenism, condescension, exclusion, and even silliness deriving from discomfort with the female "intruder."

Emily knows that the partner who made the comment that made her feel like a token rather than a member of the group had no idea what Emily was thinking at that moment. "I could have crawled under the table. It was like 'Hello everyone, she's a woman.'" Although Emily is certain that "he'd be so hurt if he thought that he had upset me," she reluctantly concludes, "They're just clueless. They're totally clueless. And it's just so frustrating. It's as if they constantly have to point out that you're female. I just don't get it. I'm not sitting there thinking of them as 'male.'"

Even though Emily is a major contributor in her firm, she has found that assumptions about gender make a difference in how senior management views people there. One explanation might be that these men are not working directly with her on a daily basis, but somehow they always seem to know what the young men are doing. At a meeting to discuss firm publicity, David*, a partner, gave a brief career synopsis for everyone sitting around the conference table. As Emily recalls, "He gave a little spiel about how wonderful each of the men is, offering comments like 'Bob is a corporate and securities lawyer. He just closed this great public offering.'"

When it was time to introduce her, instead of saying, "Emily is a corporate and securities lawyer and is involved in a lot of high-profile public mortgage-backed securities deals," he announced, "Emily takes a lot of great vacations." Emily at first thought, "I have taken some great vacations, but what does that have to do with my skills as a lawyer?" What she later said out loud after the meeting was over, with both strength and humor in her tone of voice was: "David, what is this? Diss-the-woman-lawyer morning?"

David apologized to Emily, but she doesn't think he really "got it." Although Emily has decided not to let such moments bring her down, she is determined to minimize their frequency—for her and all her female colleagues. As she walked into her next meeting with David, she reminded him, still with humor, "You're not going to insult me today, are you?" And he didn't.

APPROPRIATE RESPONSE TO INAPPROPRIATE BEHAVIOR

When Catherine Lee became partner at a midsized Portland, Maine, law firm, she started an annual ritual—a dinner for all the women at the firm to counteract the absence of a critical mass and to support women moving up the ranks. Surprisingly, this one event generated an unbelievable amount of controversy among the men. "How would you like it if we went out and did that?" they asked. Although Catherine didn't respond, she couldn't help but think "Of course, you do it every noontime, but nobody even notices."

At one of their first dinners, Catherine and eleven female colleagues rented a small restaurant. They were just sitting down for drinks and socializing when a group of men from the firm "crashed" the dinner. As Catherine recalls, "Grown-up men, partners, and associates just showed up and said, 'Here we are, girls.' We were embarrassed. It was awkward." After the men had a drink, they went home, but their contentious behavior did not stop there.

When a police officer arrived at the restaurant, the women were once again reminded of how threatened their male colleagues felt by the rarely seen women-only business gathering. With a laugh, Catherine recounts, "Given the earlier events, everybody assumed this guy must be a male stripper sent by the men in the firm. As it turned out, he was an honest-to-goodness police officer from a town the firm represents, and he served us with this fake complaint some of the men had put together for engaging in 'sexist' behavior."

After the dinner, there was much discussion among the women about how to respond and indeed whether to respond at all to the uninvited guests from the firm. Catherine and her colleagues were concerned about how to react to this rather unexpected challenge from their male peers and, in some cases, from the men who were their bosses. "We didn't want to seem shrill. We didn't want to be labeled as bitches who have no sense of humor, especially when you have to face them at 9 the next morning."

For one brief evening, the men in the office found the tables turned, and, for this, they felt threatened and excluded by the women's socializing. Recognizing that many of the men in the firm are not yet comfortable working side by side with them, the women decided to take the high—and politically wise—road and not bring up the dinner incident back at work.

While the lines that define the relationship barriers between men and women at work are typically drawn more subtly than this crashing-the-party example, this seemingly minor yet highly symbolic incident captures the dilemma professional women face every day: What do you do when someone confronts you with unacceptable behavior ranging from the quietly contentious to the blatantly hostile? How do you respond?

Part of Catherine's regular routine includes walking into depositions where six men are sitting around a table. She joins them, and then another lawyer comes in and says, "Good morning, gentlemen." Catherine describes this phenomenon as "sort of routinely being invisible" and adds, "It's a little thing, but it gets to you after a while." These are the kinds of workplace slights that most women simply choose to ignore.

For the most part, Catherine recognizes this discomfort for what it is: a basic resistance to accepting women as equal partners in business. Every once in awhile, Catherine goes into a female colleague's office, closes the door tightly, and says, "I am so sick of this b.s. You know? It really takes a lot of patience."

Catherine has observed a wide range of responses to gender bias. "There are some women who become 'one of the guys'" she says. "There are some women who come in here 'nose to the grindstone' and keep their heads down to avoid any kind of controversy; there are some who are outspoken; there are others who are slowly trying to change the system while just doing their jobs."

Determined not to let gender barriers wear her down or diminish her professional integrity, Catherine has recalibrated her perspective on change. "I've modified somewhat my response to what I perceive as inequities, frustrations, and obstacles. In the past, I was more likely to come out with guns blazing on every issue. But I found that that approach often didn't work. It was more effective for me to work behind the scenes in certain situations."

Sarah Curran attributes some men's discomfort with a woman's business success to a core male fear of a woman's professional potential. "I think the fear comes from the 50 percent of the population that used to be in control now seeing that the competition has just doubled. So their whole power base is being diluted, just by sheer numbers if nothing else. I guess if that were happening to me, I could be intimidated too."

Sarah believes the best hope for closing the gender divide at work lies in the attitude of the new managerial woman. "We don't have to climb over people in order to win," she explains. "It seems to me that each person's success is probably fairly independent of others anyway. I think it is more natural for most women to be collaborative rather than competitive. Being successful at somebody else's expense doesn't feel like a complete victory."

THE SPORTS MENTALITY

Businessmen have traditionally attached high value to the socializing that takes place on the golf course, at the local restaurant bar, in the gym locker room. Understandably, these business rituals evolved out of the friendships that are formed among colleagues at work. And these personal relationships often heighten trust in a business setting. Unfortunately, when the colleagues include a woman, the informal rules for business socializing often don't adjust to include her.

To golf or not to golf is a subject of great debate among many women. Some women believe that golfing is critical to gaining the ear of clients and bosses. Others wonder why so much business seems destined to be managed on the golf course. Cynthia Friend, a pioneer chemist and the first woman to receive tenure in the chemistry department at Harvard, finds women unwelcome on the golf course even when they are excellent players.

Whenever she travels to a professional conference, Cynthia golfs from the men's tees so that she can play with someone at her skill level. This, she says, "really bugs them." On one occasion, she was paired with some men she had never met. According to *Harvard Magazine*, "When they realized she was hitting the ball as far as they were, they started to swing harder and faster. 'If you've ever played golf, you know that's absolutely the wrong thing to do,' says Friend. 'You lose your timing and you won't hit anything.' The men got worse with every hole and started going into water and into the trees. They quit on the sixth hole. 'It was hilarious,' says Friend."[1]

Sarah Curran admits that she went through a phase early in her career when she thought that pretending to be interested in sports would strengthen her business contacts: "I would read the sports pages just so that I knew what was going on. Otherwise, I wouldn't even know who played in the Super Bowl, much less who won, because I didn't care. I don't do that anymore."

Another senior woman, in a banking specialty where her clients are accustomed to be being invited to sports events, avoids her own discomfort—as well as perceptions of impropriety as a single woman—by inviting her primarily male clients (and a guest of their choice) to dinner and theater events. She has noticed other women at the bank taking her lead now that she has found good alternatives to the hockey arena and the late-night pub.

Much has been written to suggest that early male socialization—around sports and competition—sets the stage for a highly aggressive "I win/you lose" business attitude that doesn't sit well with most women. Many of those I spoke with described how a sports orientation, conveyed in male codes of workplace conduct, shuts them out of one more level of organizational acceptance.

Andrea Stevens*, one of only three senior-partner women in a large New York law firm, tells the story of a meeting with a new client. "I remember thinking," she chuckles, "this is doomed to failure. Frequently throughout the meeting, the men would leave the room and high-five each other outside. These were my clients. And I thought, 'I'm supposed to gain their confidence, yet I can't relate to the fact that every time they think they've won a point, they excuse themselves to go out in the hallway or to the men's room and congratulate each other.'" The message sent to women through behavior like this is: "I'm in. She's out. We men have to stick together."

As long as professional men equate teamwork with a football game and treat business negotiations with a locker-room mentality, women may continue to feel isolated from important career opportunities. They notice the many ways in which this mentality separates the girls from the boys in junior high and the men from the women in corporate America.

Relationship Building and the Gender Advantage

When Wall Street's Marianne Bye first started her career in finance fifteen years ago, she noticed that many senior men helped her because they seemed to view her as they would a daughter in business. In hindsight, she sees some of their behavior as paternalistic. Since those days, she has observed few changes in how differently women and men are treated when they walk in the corporate door with identical credentials. "I see a smart woman who's 25 come in to see top management, and they still think of her as a cute young girl. Behind the scenes, everyone is checking her out. The interviewing manager may or may not have high expectations, whereas when a young man walks in, management is more likely to see what he's made of and ask aggressive questions." This is an example of how a man can find a gender advantage even at the early stages of his career.

Women in fields ranging from finance and law to manufacturing and insurance report that it is often easier to forge alliances with clients than with colleagues in their own organizations. As Marianne explains, "I find that client service is something that women are very good at. I don't know whether it's because we're not particularly intimidating or because we're always willing to help people. I get a lot of business by bringing an investor up to speed on industry trends because I can, in a very nonintimidating way, teach him the ropes." In marked contrast, she says, "Many of the men I work with come across as having big egos when they, in so many words, say: 'This is the best stock. You better buy it. If you don't, you're a fool.'"

Marianne attributes this difference in style to relying on providing information to build relationships versus relying on "muscle." She also points to the weakness in depending on machismo to win confidence: "The truth is that when you rely on bravado too much, you are eventually wrong. And people can't wait to get you when you're down. One of my competitors is all muscle. And he's often wrong. I have seen many unsuspecting investors burned."

To solidify trust with her clients, Marianne says, "I have never been a big loud voice, but I've been right on my stocks and I'm approachable. I think that maybe the reason I've done well is that I have less of an 'in-your-face' and more of a teaching orientation."

Sometimes, *not* being perceived as a threat opens unlikely business doors for women. Woman after woman echoed the experience of Catherine Lee: "Many of my clients open up to me and talk about their personal lives. And I think that has something to do with being a woman. This connection makes it more pleasant to work together. It's an advantage that works to the benefit of the client as well."

Feeling themselves in a less adversarial position, clients are more likely to reveal their business vulnerabilities and to admit what they don't know. This openness is advantageous to the firm as well. As Catherine explains, "In today's legal market, it's extremely important to be able to maintain clients because the business is so competitive. And I think women tend to be better at relationships, more sensitive to what's really important to people. I'm not saying there aren't men who are good at that, but I think that most women have been brought up to be more attuned to what people really want."

College administrator Mary McAteer Kennedy believes that education through example is a powerful learning tool for both men and women. As director of dining services, she supervises a large male staff and recognizes an advantage in their style. "They're more direct when they are upset and the staff knows it; I tend, on the other hand, to put off bad news a bit longer or am more subtle about how I approach it. I could see that this style of mine was less effective than theirs. I've changed my style; I'm more direct about addressing problems now." Mary believes early socialization explains some of the differences in management style: "We've been trained not to alienate people, not to start a fight, to keep everything on an even keel and in control. Sometimes, in order to get to that point, you just have to grin and bear it and deal with the problems immediately—so that you can move on."

Mary's staff appreciates the strengths that she, as a woman, has brought to managing their department. "The men who work for me say that the biggest difference in having a woman boss—and the one they appreciate the most—is that I don't fly off the handle the way most of their male bosses do. They don't have to deal with the stress of having a boss who reacts to problems by getting loud and abusive."

ADDING VALUE FOR YOUR BOSS

One of the most critical workplace alliances is the one you develop with your boss. The higher a woman rises, the more likely it is that her boss will be a man. Mary McAteer Kennedy's current job tells the classic story of a woman tested by a crusty older boss who had never before worked with a female manager.

When Mary applied for a job with Larry, he had just taken over as a department head, having worked his way up the career ladder through thirty years in the business. In the interview process itself, Larry made it clear that his first choice for the job was a man who had restaurant, rather than management, experience. What finally won Larry over, after a third interview at the insistence of his boss, was that Mary knew the precise formula for making mayonnaise. As it turned out, she had worked in a hospital kitchen as a high-school student where, she recalls, "I had to make mayonnaise every Saturday from scratch—ten gallons of mayonnaise—carefully drizzling in just the right amount of oil."

On one level, it seemed silly to Mary that such a small detail should finally grab Larry's attention. On another, it signaled that it would be up to her—not him—to overcome the differences in training and management style that might inhibit a productive alliance. When Mary began working for Larry, she carefully analyzed how their skills might complement one another. Once Larry got beyond the gender issue, he realized Mary's strength and ability to help him with the legalities of dealing with labor issues. In return, he could teach her how to deal with a male crew of electricians, plumbers, and cooks who were not accustomed to accepting direction from a woman.

By coaching Mary on thorny questions the tradespeople would raise with her, Larry cemented Mary's loyalty and support. When the staff didn't like Mary's response, they would look to Larry for a different answer, and he would simply say: "You heard her." After seeing that Mary could hold her ground consistently, the staff found it easier just to be straight with her when a problem arose.

While there are few situations where knowing the secret to good mayonnaise will land you a job in upper-middle management, Mary's example points to a key strategy for relationship-building when a potential male boss cannot perceive of a woman supervising a primarily male staff. Since most people tend to groom and promote who they know and who they understand, gender at first clouded Larry's ability to see Mary's management potential. Understanding that, Mary set out to build their relationship by looking at the skills each brought to the table.

Mary has always tried to watch her bosses to find out what it was that they *didn't* want to do. In a previous job, after she noticed that the budget process took her boss away from long-range planning, Mary volunteered to take responsibility for one budget area. Little by little, she took on more and more of the budget work. When Mary noticed that personnel management and dealing with the labor union seemed both time-consuming and tedious to her boss, she said, "Whatever you want me to do in personnel, just give it to me." Eventually Mary was doing all the personnel management.

Mary concentrated on outcomes that made her boss look good to the organization. This made it possible for her to aggressively seek new opportunities to enhance her managerial skills without causing her boss to feel threatened by her initiative and ambition.

ASSERTING YOUR INDEPENDENCE

Once a women passes a certain learning curve, asserting her independence from a male boss is essential if she is to avoid a career dead end. One can't stay in a helper role for too long. Catherine Lee has noticed that "It's not unusual for a woman, at some point in her career, to be the woman behind the man who keeps the client happy day-to-day while he is off doing sixteen other things.

Some women reject that role earlier than others and grow into their independence. Others stay with it and become very frustrated."

As she moved along the partnership track, Catherine carefully benchmarked the development of her relationship with her boss. "It was, at times, like having another marriage. I'd have to go in every three months and have this serious talk about how we were doing. But the relationship grew, and he never stood in the way of my advancement."

As Catherine cautions, "I've seen women not claim their independence, not take the initiative to get out from under the protection that can at first be good. They end up being very angry once they realize they really can do more, but the men continue to take advantage of them as a subordinate." The young male associates, Catherine observes, tend not to stay under someone's wing; they break out faster from being the behind-the-scenes person. This is probably due, in part, to their own socialization and, in part, to a male boss who deliberately pushes his male protégé out of the nest.

TEAMS AND SHARING CREDIT

Visibility—or lack of it—is directly linked to opportunities for building productive alliances. Chemistry professor Cynthia Friend advises her female colleagues to "make sure you get credit for the job that you do. It will help in relationship-building." Again and again, the women I surveyed pointed to situations where they noticed a marked difference in how their male colleagues shared, or didn't share, credit for a group effort. Many women described situations where their male colleagues seemed to feel the need to hoard credit rather than recognize contributions of other members on their team.

A man's level of comfort with a female colleague does not always improve over time. When Catherine Lee became a firm partner, her male colleagues began to view her as "the competition." The first time she brought in a big client on her own, Catherine observed an about-face in how many of the men treated her. One male partner, whom Catherine had considered a friend, began to spread the word that Catherine was not, in fact, the deal closer who landed the client. What disturbed Catherine most—more than his blatant distortion of the facts—was his deliberate attack on her professional success.

At first Catherine was appalled that someone with whom she thought she had a good working relationship would try to sabotage her success. Then she realized, "There is nearly constant insecurity in this practice if you haven't got a big case or if you're not in the middle of a big trial or if you haven't just won a big verdict. It's as if you've never done anything. There's nonstop pressure to achieve something very significant—so anybody else's accomplishments just escalate this pressure."

Whether the attempt to sabotage her success was gender-based or merely an example of the aggressive male style of her firm—or a little of both—Catherine is promoting alternatives to such demonstrations of professional insecurity. She believes in a long-term view on the value of sharing business credit. "Typically, in our bonus system, the primary attorney gets the bonus and it's entirely up to that person whether to share it with anybody. I've always felt that it's important to share the credit even though I work with lawyers who won't do the same thing." As part of her educational approach to changing the traditional rules, Catherine tries to convey to the men in her office that being fair in sharing credit is more important to her than the extra money she would receive for hoarding it.

For women at the associate level, Catherine has noticed that the only people who were given a share of the bonuses by senior men were those who walked into their boss's office and said, "You know, I really am entitled to a portion of this bonus." Catherine herself was an exception. The first time she took over a big case on her own, her boss announced, "This is all yours. You earned it. You can take the credit." Most senior men, Catherine believes, are not this generous because, she believes, "When a woman reaches a certain level of achievement, she's no longer perceived as person who needs to be encouraged. She's now the competition."

31

Packaging Business Language

Effective business language requires finding the right tools to introduce a concept and to bring it to professional recognition. One persuasive strategy, often used by men, involves "packaging" the ideas they present in a meeting or at a professional conference: taking the floor to first introduce the concept, often with a good business story; then listing key points; and, finally, wrapping it up with a strong closing statement. Women can certainly package their ideas in the same fashion but face one barrier—they are more likely to be interrupted when they take control of the floor.

Critical mass can often determine who is heard and who isn't. Catherine Lee has noticed a change in her own outlook since there are more female partners in her firm: "There are six of us now, so I don't feel that I'm alone so much anymore. It's not that my women colleagues are necessarily outspoken; it's just that it's a different environment now. I walk into a partners' meeting and see six women sitting there as opposed to three."

Cynthia Friend also notices the change at work. The vast majority of the time she is comfortable in asserting her right to be heard, but this is even more so now that she has tenure at her university. "I am fairly aggressive about asking questions. If someone tries to interrupt me in a meeting, I won't let them. I'll say, 'I'm going to finish. Please raise that comment later.' If someone repeats something I said, I'll say something like 'Oh, I'm glad you agree with the point I just made. That's exactly what I was just saying five minutes ago.'"

Cynthia admits that there can be a fine line between being heard and being heard too much. "If I get upset about something, I have a tendency to talk too much, to use too many words to say the same thing. It's more effective to choose words carefully and be assertive and crisp in what you say. Intonation and body language can be used forcefully too."

Cynthia suggests that effective business conversation finds its origins in confidence and offers this advice: "You have to believe in what you're going to say and not be afraid to say it. The hardest thing for anyone to learn is that everyone says something that could be construed as stupid sometimes. But you can't worry about that. And in reality, no one will think ill of you unless you're saying stupid things all the time."

As confident as Cynthia is, even she admits to occasional lapses into the "good-girl syndrome" rather than taking a conversational risk. As she explains, "I sometimes feel like I have to fit into a neat slot—feeling like I should go along with certain things I don't agree with. But fortunately, that feeling doesn't last very long!"

BRIDGING THE RELATIONSHIP GAP

All the principles for gender equity that you'll be reading about in the rest of this book are founded on good relationships between women and men and between women and their organizations. The most successful women I spoke with have already figured this out for themselves. Here are some of the strategies that have worked for them:

- Adopt a big-picture view on bridging the gender gap. Ignore the battles not worth fighting with individuals who offer no hope for change.

- Seize opportunities to enlighten the men in your office who are open to change. When you find yourself an outsider to insider conversations, make the first move to join in. When appropriate, use humor to make a point and hopefully to educate a less-than-enlightened colleague.

- Counteract invisibility by finding opportunities for your business skills to be noticed. Volunteer for high-visibility projects and important committees. Identify and build your own business niche to open the doors for professional recognition. Make your business vision heard by experimenting with strategies for effective business style and presentation. Ask bosses and trusted colleagues for honest feedback.

33

- When male business bonding excludes you, particularly in after-hour forums, take charge of your own career and concentrate on outcomes that carry a high value to your boss and your organization. Figuring out what adds value to your organization offers a key point of entry to building productive business relationships.

- Be creative in establishing new traditions for client entertainment: lunch meetings, family events, opportunities at professional conferences. Invite the men in your office to join you.

- Help your organization break out of an exclusionary macho mentality by demonstrating new models for collegiality: speak up in meetings with a clear focus on business; recognize the contributions of everyone who contributes to a work team; break out of support roles into line positions where you can assert a new, inclusive managerial tone.

- Step forward with new models for collaboration that recognize that women and men can learn from each other's strengths. When in doubt, take the high road in dealing with a hostile colleague. The women I surveyed told me it pays off in the long run.

CHAPTER 3

TAKING RISKS

"Removing gender barriers at entry and middle levels would give women a chance to perform—to demonstrate competence—with little risk to the organization. The greater challenge is the next step—opening the doors to senior-level women who have already succeeded at lower levels. Once that occurs, women need the same 'freedom to fail' that is accorded men—allowing them to take risks that result in higher payoff for the company."

—Anne Clark*, a senior vice president in corporate lending

Successful careers require risk-taking. How much does the *ability* to take risks rely on gender? The answer is: very little.

But a complicated set of stereotypes surrounds women and risk. What woman after woman told me—from observing others and from personal experience—is that the woman who takes on the high-risk assignment is watched more closely than the man who does the same thing. If she does well, her success—perhaps a surprise to some—is more likely to be noticed among predominantly male peers. If, on the other hand, a woman comes up against a setback, she puts her career momentum in serious jeopardy—a scenario not usually faced by men who stumble every once in awhile.

35

The woman is judged by one standard: "She doesn't have what it takes." The man is judged by another: "He didn't make it *this* time, but I give him credit for his gutsy style."

These different standards for risk-taking begin with the messages many of us receive from our parents and teachers at an early age. The young girl who climbs a high tree is told to come down right away; the little boy in the tree is left alone to explore and play. Girls are encouraged to be concerned about safety, about getting along, about not making too many waves. Boys are coached to challenge their physical limits, demonstrate leadership potential, and stir up activity.

Matina Horner, former president of Radcliffe College, was one of the first to suggest that women fear success because they assume a collision between the traits associated with power and the attributes expected from women. Fully comfortable with the skills and stamina requisite to risk-taking but aware of the high career penalty carried by women who stumble, a woman has good reason to think twice about a speculative business move. Among the women I met, the barriers they face are institutional, not personal.

Opportunities for risk-taking are often closed to women. Fifty-four percent of the women in my survey believe that being a woman limits opportunities to take on high-visibility assignments and almost this same number believe it has limited their opportunity to take career risks. Not surprisingly, women already in senior management perceived fewer obstacles to risk-taking. They have, perhaps, taken enough chances in their careers to have developed personal comfort with the notion of occasional professional failure, knowing that they can still succeed over the long-term.

Opportunity for the high-risk, high-visibility assignment often begins with support from a boss or mentor. Informal sponsorship by a senior colleague or boss, a built-in career benefit for many men, can support a high-risk project by alerting a risk-taker to political landmines and by finding business alliances to support the venture.

A 1992 Korn/Ferry survey of 400 senior business women identified risk-taking as a key factor in their career advancement. Seventy-one percent of these executive women have taken risks to gain visibility and accelerate career momentum. Thirty-six percent said that taking on a high-risk project marked a turning point for their career success.[1]

All trailblazers carry risks. A woman's first risk as a trailblazer begins with the hiring process. Knowing that she will be watched closely, particularly when she is selected over a predominantly male candidate pool, heightens the responsibility she feels to do well. And when she is the first or only woman in the job, the visibility places her at risk. Many of the women I surveyed described two layers of success—first, in the rewards of their own careers and, second, in the doors they are opening for the women who will follow them. Being cast as role models can carry a rich reward as well as a heavy burden. If they do not do well, it will be harder for the next woman to succeed.

The women in this chapter describe how they transformed what is euphemistically termed a "learning experience" into a professional opportunity. They offer strategies for assuming risks on the job—ranging from taking conversational risks in a roomful of men to making bold and courageous professional moves.

The Courage to Make Unpopular Decisions

Carole St. Mark offers this perspective on knowing when to take an unpopular stand: "Don't take on issues that are purely personal. It quickly becomes clear to people that you're fighting for your own ego or your own turf. Any battles you fight ought to be for the good of the company. Not that you shouldn't fight for your position when necessary—you should. But ego can take people down faster than anything else."

Wall Street's Carolynn Rockafellow agrees. A managing director at First Boston Corporation, she consistently positions the risks she takes in her own career in the broader context of doing what is best for the firm. And this strategy has enabled her to advance in an industry known for being less than hospitable to women.

Using her thirteen years of institutional credibility to minimize career fallout from the risks she chooses to take, Carolynn observes, "I think most women are very risk adverse. I've always had a perspective in my career—which is not necessarily the safest—that it's my job as a partner to tell the truth about what I see and how I think the business could run better. And that means taking some pretty big risks. But in return I'm seen as someone who gets the job done."

Carolynn has gone through periods of not being the most popular of managers because she's backed a controversial decision and faced harsh criticism from her colleagues. She acknowledges, "It's much nicer if everyone is friends," but, "that's not what we're here to do."

Conventional business wisdom suggests that taking risks involves making some tough and unpleasant business decisions. Carolynn describes the realistic attitude she has developed that, admittedly, sounds harsher coming from a woman than from a man at the senior executive level: "I'm not here for someone to like me or not like me. I'm here to do my job. I'm not very personal about my approach to people who are trying to do a job with me because they're either doing a good job or they're not. This approach works for me, but I think it's very hard for some women to adopt it themselves."

Carolynn has noticed that when she delivers messages about performance, many women seem to take criticism more personally than the men. "It seems to be easier for the men to accept. Maybe men just have more self-esteem. It seems a lot easier for men to separate criticism from who they are as people." Pointing to how personally many women take setbacks, Carolynn says, "I think that makes it very hard for women not to get bogged down in self-criticism, self-blame, and self-questioning rather than just moving on when someone doesn't think they did a good job." This may explain why some women may find it more comfortable to play it safe, particularly when they are already under greater scrutiny than the men in the office.

Many of the women who responded to my survey observed that men are more comfortable in deflecting blame for a setback on the job, letting go of what is out of their control. As a rule, men will blame the team, an off day, or even bad luck; women, on the other hand, take it all home, carrying the guilt on a personal level.

Carolynn is so clear about putting aside personal motivation in the best interest of the firm that, in 1994, she took the ultimate career risk, developing a business plan that eliminated her own job. When a new company president asked to see all the managing directors one-by-one to get to know them, Carolynn seized the opportunity for making a radical proposal. "I went in with a plan for dissolving my group. Although I thought our group did a terrific job, I didn't think it made a lot of sense in the way we had to funnel the product through the new organization."

Although the group's break-up was very sensitive politically, Carolynn's goal was to simplify the process for customers and reduce the firm's overhead costs. "I did work myself out of a job. My main concern was that I could reposition the people in my group—who were all tremendous producers—in departments where they could make an impact and have job security." She achieved her goal: Everyone in her group landed good jobs, and Carolynn herself moved into another managing director slot.

Accepting risk involves accepting occasional failure. Women who have broken through the gender barriers in their organizations, taking risks along the way, think like this: "What's the worst that can happen if I don't succeed on this project? If things don't go as planned, what's my first move to get back on track?"

Many of the women I met have learned, quite deliberately, to take a long-term view of the peaks and valleys in their careers. A less personalized outlook on criticism and professional failures fortifies them so they're not derailed by professional setbacks.

JUMPSTARTING A CAREER

Careers plateau for a variety of reasons. Flatter, leaner, and meaner organizations restrict upward career mobility for many talented people. And in an uncertain economy, anyone, woman or man, may find it safer to stick with a sure thing. When Carol Goldberg found her career stalled in a traditionally "female" career slot, she took a careful look at where the rising stars came from in the

Stop & Shop retail chain. She remembers asking herself, "Who is going to the top? Only the people with sales and operating experience. And where was I? Doing a great job in marketing. Was I going to get to the top from marketing? No way!"

Carol almost fell into the trap of doing what her colleagues thought was right for her—the "but everybody loves what you do" rationale for *not* leaving a job. Carol's typically no-nonsense assessment of this well-intentioned, but strategically poor, advice was "Too bad. It's wonderful to be so good in marketing, but it doesn't match my ambition."

After eight years in marketing, Carol realized that she was "peaking out," becoming dangerously comfortable in her job. It took three years of planning to position herself for a major career transition, clearing the decks for her husband to take over on the home front and preparing for a sublateral career move to a new specialty within the organization.

To send the clear signal that she was launching a significant career change, Carol first entered a three-month advanced management program at Harvard Business School. "I wanted to ensure that everyone in my family and in senior management understood that I was not returning to my job," she says.

Carol felt strongly that she first needed to go backward to reposition her career, in part because she faced the issue of proving herself in a family-owned business and, more importantly, because she wanted to develop credibility within a new segment of the company. So she took a position in the Stop & Shop-owned Bradlees store chain "way down in operations in an apparel merchandising job." Her responsibilities included supervision of six New England stores. "I didn't have a fancy title. I didn't have a fancy office. My office was in the trunk of my car as I drove from store to store, but I was deliriously happy."

Carol found her skills stretched and her learning curve steep, both of which revived her career. In her previous job, she only had to mine creativity from small groups of people. In the field, Carol says, supervisory skills carry higher stakes. "I lived in a goldfish bowl. The employees watched every step and every move I made. They watched how I acted with the store manager and the department managers."

The challenge for Carol was in learning to be "able to communicate with lots of people you can't spend a lot of time with. With several hundred people in each store, I could not speak to each person. I had to learn how to communicate my values efficiently and effectively."

Carol's sublateral career move to a line function paid off, allowing her to rise steadily through the ranks at Stop & Shop to president and chief operating officer.

Taking the Plunge

Sarah Curran*, a vice president at a large manufacturing firm, proposes a strategy, admittedly risky and controversial, that she sometimes uses for asserting her business value. When there are seemingly endless—and artificial—reasons for her not to take the plunge into a risky situation, Sarah tells herself, "Don't ask permission now. Just beg forgiveness later."

Sarah cites as an example a recent meeting of all her company's officers to review their executive compensation system. "Everybody was in town that day because the purpose of the meeting was for us to give input on what we thought about the existing executive compensation system and how we might change it. We were all at risk because any suggestions we came up with could potentially cut into your own pockets."

Not surprisingly, the discussion was very low-key until Sarah broke the silence with a controversial proposal: "Why don't we restructure the way we award bonuses? As we now have it set up, 80 percent of all our bonuses is virtually guaranteed. Why isn't the whole bonus at risk? Why doesn't anyone ever get a zero bonus? Or 120 percent?"

At one point in the meeting, as Sarah engaged in a one-on-one conversation with the outside compensation expert, she was so totally focused on the content that she tuned out the talk around her. For a brief moment, Sarah wondered if she was talking too much. "It was risky," she says, "but I'm at the bottom of the totem pole. What do I have to lose? It's riskier for those higher up who just got into 'the club.'"

For Sarah, showcasing her analytic skills was a way for her to send another message to senior management. "I'm not afraid to take a risk in this organization." In Sarah's case, this was a gamble that yielded immediate professional recognition and new access to the ears of senior management. "I've noticed that a few of the officers who normally wouldn't give me the time of day started to spend time with me following that meeting."

Floating a controversial business idea can, at one extreme, diminish credibility for someone not truly accepted by the inner circle. And it can be difficult to make your ideas known if your style is different from most other people in the room. But the potential payoff may well be worth taking this chance. The ability to successfully take the plunge into risky business situations is predicated on behaving as though it is within the span of your authority to do so. And then, Sarah suggests, "People start to believe in you."

Like Sarah Curran, Catherine Lee already has a strong track record behind her, and she finds that she can take the kinds of risks that would have seemed too high when she was being evaluated for partnership. Now that she has some measure of job security, she says, "I don't feel any significant risk in doing what I feel is right—although I realize that others may perceive me as a troublemaker for standing up for what I believe in."

Taking a Stand

Anne Clark*, a senior vice president in corporate lending, has made a conscious effort never to do anything that would label her as a "whiner" in her almost exclusively male environment. But she chose to take a firm stand when a man at her level, whom she had consistently outperformed, was promoted into her boss's position. "I had outperformed him every year—in terms of loan growth and other quantitative measures. And then I heard from someone I trusted that the chairman had made the comment that I am too pretty to collect loans."

For about six months, Anne lived with the aggravation of having many of the staff members come to her, rather than their new boss, for advice and direction. Anne admits, "He was a nice guy, but he wasn't a manager. So I was working 70 to 80 hours a week trying to run the place he couldn't run. And I was burning out with no rewards for it." She walked into the bank president's office and said, "I resign."

Over the years, Anne had seen many men threaten to quit as they touted another job offer, really using the offer as leverage to stay in the organization but in a better job. In her own case, she said, game-playing was not on her agenda. "I wasn't kidding around. I wasn't doing it to bargain for another job. I didn't even have time to look for another job because I was working so hard. I resigned because I was at the end of my rope. I said, this is insane. I'm 32 years old and too young to burn out."

As it turned out, taking a stand was the right thing for her to do. The bank president took immediate action when he realized he was about to lose a star performer. A man in another department was about to be fired, so the president moved Anne into his executive position where she has since been promoted into her current job.

Cutting Your Losses

Everyone gets knocked down at some point in their career. How they handle these setbacks determines which direction they head when they get back up.

Knowing when to cut professional losses minimizes career damage in the long run. Attitude determines how soon you get back on your feet. As Carol Goldberg suggests, "Until you understand that the risk of leaving a job is not failure, it's a bigger risk to stay where you've become a victim than it is to leave. If you don't leave, because perhaps you desperately need the money, what you do is to mentally leave. You never tell anybody you are leaving." Instead, she recommends, you should separate yourself emotionally from a bad situation while actively seeking a better job.

"The human being has a lot of leverage," says Carol. When a close friend, a senior executive, called Carol to say how miserable and underutilized she felt in her current job, Carol responded bluntly, "That's your own fault. Get out of there!" While Carol does not advocate jeopardizing your paycheck, she does believe a shift in attitude can give you the boost you need to find another job.

Beth Evans* is an engineer who has willingly tackled many of the barriers faced by women in her profession, but she has learned to recognize when battles are unwinnable. Worried that her career was plateauing, Beth scheduled a meeting with her boss and said, "Here's what I'd like to do next. I've noticed male colleagues with my same background moving into these positions. What do I need to work on to be considered for this type of job?" Her boss responded, "Don't worry. You're doing everything right. There's no problem. Just keep doing what you're doing."

Soon after this, a manager from another part of the company, "typically more female than engineering," tried to persuade Beth to join them. Beth's immediate response was "I appreciate your offer, but I want to move up on the engineering side of the business." The manager then essentially scolded Beth for her naiveté. "Look around you." she suggested. "Do you see any women in those positions here? Doesn't that tell you something?"

Beth then thought about other talented women whose morale and performance began to head in a downward spiral when they stayed in an unwinnable situation for too long. Being a trailblazer in this company, she concluded, was probably a no-win goal. She firmly believes, "Unless you really want to do battle, people's minds have to be broadened first."

To keep her career moving, Beth went to work for a competitor company with a track record for promoting talented women. She now advises others, "If you decide to fight a really bad political situation, it probably won't work and you'll get a bad reputation that could end your career. Rather than do that, I think it sends a better message to go somewhere else where you can make a difference."

When your profession encompasses a relatively small business community, the risk of fighting unwinnable battles and being branded a "troublemaker" may be too steep. Women like Beth focus not only on career advancement but on career survival as well. And they have adopted the confident view that it is the organization's loss, not their own, when it does not welcome and accept them.

A Battle Worth Fighting

Katherine Dresdner has never shied away from a professional challenge. When she entered the almost exclusively male club of plaintiff attorneys, she would, on most days, be the only woman at the court's morning calendar call. Judges would ask if she were a client and if she were "really a lawyer." Some of the older judges did not hesitate to ask if she had passed the bar.

To enhance her professional credibility, Katherine decided to go through the process of being certified as a civil trial attorney— essentially a stamp of approval for her skills in a field dominated by men. "Because of the experience I was having with men treating me like I didn't exist, I decided to apply for certification as soon as I was qualified." During her pregnancy with her daughter, Katherine passed the process that included recommendations from adversaries and judges as well as a written examination. In so doing, she became the ninth woman ever to be certified in New Jersey.

Katherine's career seemed to be humming along with a steady stream of high-profile jury verdicts in her clients' favor, including the highest award ever won by her firm. But that, she says, was the point when her law firm began to treat her differently from her all-male peers, excluding her from business strategy meetings and giving her only problem cases. "When I began to do better than any of the male attorneys, including the senior partner who was a trial lawyer, they started to shut me out." At the time she won their largest verdict, the only comment from a senior partner was "Why didn't you get more, Katherine?"

One night at 6 p.m., the firm's partners assigned Katherine a case, opened by another attorney, for trial the next day. When Katherine reviewed the case that night, she discovered serious problems with its preparation, but the judge would not agree to her request for a delay. Forced to try the case blind, with missing components to the file, she lost the case. Frustrated by being put in this untenable situation, she called a senior partner to say, "Look, I was just sandbagged. I was given this file marked ready four days in a row by another attorney, but it was absolutely not ready." Back at the firm, Katherine spoke up about what she viewed as sabotage to her career and to the client. "This is essentially malpractice," she said. "The client should not have lost the case."

Soon after this, Katherine was told by a senior partner that she was being put on probation and would not be given the lump sum bonus that normally accounted for about half her annual compensation. When a partner told her, "You have a lousy track record," Katherine headed straight for the firm's accountant. She asked for another meeting with the partner, where she presented the facts about her contribution to the firm. "I brought the records of all the money I had brought in, but it didn't matter. They just wanted me out."

Katherine felt she had no option but to resign and look for another job. After many months of personal and professional introspection, Katherine filed a lawsuit, waiting until two days before the statutory time limit to file a sex discrimination suit within the Division for Civil Rights. Aware, as a lawyer herself, of the high career penalty attached to those who seek legal remedy for gender bias, Katherine says, "I lost the chance for a jury trial by filing in the administrative courts, but I felt that I had to protect my career. I wanted to fight them, but I had to find a place to do it that would be safest for me."

In the course of the trial, one male attorney from the firm confirmed what she had suspected. Katherine was deliberately assigned the cases with so many problems that no one else wanted to touch them. And she had summarily been excluded from all the firm's social events from which business is often generated.

After two years in the court system, the firm offered Katherine a financial settlement that, while drastically lower than traditional jury awards, represented for Katherine a moral victory. Katherine wonders if the senior partner who kept her on the stand for twenty-two days will ever understand the true injustice represented in her case. Two days after the trial was settled, he started referring cases to her, despite the fact that he had testified, in court, that he believed she was unqualified for this type of work. "I can't understand his behavior," Katherine admits. "Maybe he was acknowledging that he had been wrong in the way he treated me and was trying to make up for it, but he was incredibly abusive toward me in court."

Katherine's strong track record, her belief in herself, and deeply felt convictions about bias of any sort helped her land on her feet professionally, but the court case was grueling—even for a lawyer accustomed to the process. As Katherine explains, "The case took forever. And preparing for the court appearances took huge amounts of time away from my own work. My file was 2 to 3 feet thick."

Each day in court, Katherine was forced to justify her legal credentials: educational background, details from her court cases, overall track record. And each night, after her daughter went to sleep, she would spend several hours preparing for the next day. Although she suffers occasional moments of self-doubt about the toll the trial took on her family, Katherine needed to feel personally vindicated about the legitimacy of her case. Conveying both confidence and peace of mind, she says, "I had to do it for myself. It was very important for me to stand up to the law partners. I couldn't let them step on me like that because it wasn't right."

Katherine today is part of a small law firm run as a cooperative. Her integrity is intact, her career is thriving, and she goes to sleep at night knowing that she did the right thing—for her—in summoning the courage to confront discrimination. Her story explains why so many women who face discrimination never rely on legal protection as an effective remedy. In Katherine's case, however, doing nothing would have been more devastating to her, both personally and professionally. She believes it would have seriously undermined the level of belief she has in herself, which prepares her for the long and difficult trials required by the type of law she practices.

CREATING YOUR OWN SAFETY ZONE

In the groundbreaking book *The Managerial Woman*, Margaret Hennig and Anne Jardim described how successful businesswomen felt about risk in the 1970s: "Women see risk as entirely negative. It is loss, danger, injury, ruin, hurt. One avoids it as best one can."[2]

In 1996, the women I met hold a markedly different perspective on translating risk into opportunity. They have bypassed fear of failure by adopting the view suggested by psychologist Sylvia Senter that "we learn from our mistakes, more than from our successes." And, as Senter suggests, "The higher up you are in business, the more you gamble. You win some, you lose some. My boss made plenty of mistakes too."[3]

In venturing into the territory of risk—uncharted for many women—the women I met are secure enough in their professional confidence to be able to live with the possibility of failure. To enhance their probability of success, here are some of the principles they follow:

- Trust your instincts. The highest career risk comes with not being comfortable with the merits of your ability and style. Women who take risks trust their own instincts, even under direct challenge. They are comfortable in their own skins, even when markedly different from the rest of the team.

- Choose your battles carefully. Fighting too many battles reduces your chances of winning any of them. Carolynn Rockafellow has learned that you need a lot of credibility before you can expect to win an uphill battle. "I've gotten better over the years at picking the right battles. It's too discouraging and disheartening to fight every battle. It's exhausting and you have to build your reputation. You need facts to back you up. Then it's harder for people to challenge you."

- Take a dispassionate view of your professional talents. Believing in yourself fortifies your own comfort zone for risk-taking. Few successful people have made it to the top without wins and losses in their career gambles.

- Recognize that there are times when the safest course for a career is to take a risk, make a change. As Katherine Dresdner found, not taking a stand against an extreme work situation might have derailed her entire law career.

- To counteract professional invisibility, generate opportunities for risk in the context of what makes good sense for your organization. This takes the heat off you personally while generating real potential to move your career forward.

- And remember that there is usually a cost attached to anything worth having. Taking a risk opens up potential for criticism but also potential for real reward.

CHAPTER 4

REPLACING THE DOUBLE STANDARD

"There's still a double standard in the courtroom. An assertive woman is told she's too aggressive. And yet, if you're not assertive and aggressive, you can't do your job. You have to be fearless to get up in front of a jury, present your case, and do your job well."

—Katherine Dresdner, trial attorney

The year 1995 seemed to be the year of the double standard for women in the public eye. Publicly ostracized for spending more time on the job than with her children, Marcia Clark was only doing what male trial attorneys who are also parents do day after day. The plane crash of Lt. Kara Hultgreen, the Navy's first woman fighter pilot, brought intense media scrutiny of her right to be in the plane—because of her gender alone. We learned, in the course of speculation about pilot error later dismissed by a formal Navy investigation, that Lt. Hultgreen had ranked first and second in several key flight competencies.

The assumptions behind the judgments passed on Kara Hultgreen and Marcia Clark get to the heart of the inconsistency in standards. In the case of Lt. Hultgreen, the presumption was made that she must not have been qualified to be in the pilot's seat in the first place. In reality, she was qualified and probably more motivated to succeed than many of the men on the flight deck.

Marcia Clark was simply expected to be in two places at once. No one doubted her professional abilities, but skeptics about ambitious women wondered how she could also fulfill her role as mother of two boys. Many forgot about the economic necessity of her choices, particularly the fact that she was raising her sons as a single parent.

The double standard at work extends beyond the issue of equal pay for equal work to include hiring practices, performance standards, and promotional consideration.

A disbeliever in the existence of the double standard may ask: How do women know that a double standard is the problem and not that a woman's performance is weaker?

The answer is that it is statistically improbable that every woman who is paid less than the man in the next office, who is bypassed for committee leadership or who takes longer to be made partner is simply less competent than a man. A recent year-long study of 676 male and 383 female managers, representing over 200 organizations, presents its own conclusions about women's competence: "Employees rated female managers higher than males in all twenty of the skill areas, while bosses rated females higher in nineteen of the twenty areas (technical expertise was a tie)."[1]

Evidence of the double standard is clear. Women across the country leave their offices each day earning 72 cents on the male dollar. The government's Glass Ceiling Commission found that white men with a college education were 40 percent more likely to be in managerial positions than would be expected from the number who are employed. White women in the workforce with the same educational background were underrepresented by 33 percent and black women by 12 percent.[2] Men with college degrees earn $15,000 more a year than employed women who are college educated.[3]

"When women go into traditionally male occupations, they're paid less than men are (female truck drivers, 70 cents on the man's dollar; female lawyers, 74 cents). But when men enter traditionally female occupations, they're paid more than women (male registered nurses, $1.04 on the female dollar; male office clerks, $1.09; male cashiers, $1.17)."[4]

Absent the stark reality of the numbers, women are likely to be accused of complaining or of not being a team player when they identify the inequity.

Some of the differential tracking begins in the hiring process itself. Tests for discrimination in the hiring process, where equally matched pairs of men and women are sent on job interviews, consistently report that men are much more likely to be offered a job than equally qualified women.

A Canadian study of 692 managers in a large company reported that even with controls for factors such as education and training, women were much less likely to be promoted. Another study reporting similar disadvantages in promotions revealed that women were held to higher promotion standards than men with comparable achievements.[5]

Sixty-eight percent of the women in my national sample believe they are held to a higher performance standard than their male colleagues. Only about half believe they have advanced at the same rate as men with the same credentials and abilities. The majority, including a majority of the senior managers, see gender as having limited their potential in critical career areas. Sixty-eight percent believe being a woman has held back their level of compensation; 67 percent believe it has reduced opportunities for promotions. Forty percent report that being a woman has put them at a disadvantage in being considered for leadership on committees within their organization, and 26 percent believe that gender has shut them out from leadership in professional organizations.

Just walking in the office door often carries a different set of assumptions for women and men at the same professional level. Andrea Stevens*, a senior partner in a New York law firm, describes how assumptions about gender inhibit the immediate acceptance that is accorded her male peers: "I'm regularly faced with the situation where I walk into a meeting with a male junior associate and the client automatically defers to him." The frustrations, she says, lie in the time and energy these stereotypes take away from the work that needs to get done. "You can't sit there and wave a flag and say, 'Hey, wait a second. I'm the senior partner on this transaction.' You have to make it known more gently and then wrest control of the meeting. And sometimes, you're too tired to fight it."

The double standard originates in the different set of expectations on which performance is evaluated and on which potential is judged:

Career Potential:	Let's give him a chance.
	She could use more time in this job.
Style:	He's a leader; he speaks his mind.
	She's too pushy; she always has an opinion.
Demeanor:	He's a serious guy—a hard worker.
	She has no sense of humor.
Work/Life Balance:	He has the best of both worlds.
	She's overextended.

Where does the double standard begin? At what point does it take its toll on a woman's career?

Very often, women are put at a disadvantage early on because the double standard is so pervasive. The double standard is, in fact, one standard—excused by the fact that "men and women are just different." While men are perceived to hold an intrinsic right to managerial roles, many women are merely tolerated as interlopers and bear the burden of proving that they belong in management.

Joanna Engelke, vice president at Bain & Company, a management consulting firm, describes the higher hurdles women face in developing organizational influence. "My company is very comfortable with women and has designed a set of policies more supportive of career growth (male *and* female) than other consulting firms I know of." But, she adds, "I generally find that in our clients' companies, more energy needs to be expended to find a basis for commonality, trust, and communication between women and men. It doesn't mean that all men bond really well with all other men. They don't, but there's just something about being the same gender that generally makes you bond faster." And it is this bonding among men that perpetuates the old boys' network—the underpinning for the double standard.

For a woman, perceptions about how well she has adapted to a male-defined culture play a major role in her becoming a real player in the organization. As Joanna observes, "A lot of senior women are disappointed to discover that a big part of their effectiveness is dependent upon the people they know and how they network; this fact is not a surprise to men. A smaller part—although still important—depends upon their technical ability to do a good analysis or underwrite a case correctly or make sure the budget and the production statistics are accurate."

Women like Joanna recognize that just doing good work is rarely enough to gain access to critical career opportunities. By changing the assumptions behind the double standard, they are beginning to revise business standards geared toward men.

THE SELF-FULFILLING PROPHECY

Laurie Hawkes, an investment banker in New York City, has seen time and again the double standard reveal itself on Wall Street where women comprise only 6 to 7 percent of the managing directors. But, she asserts, its origins often go back to earlier career stages.

Laurie offers the following scenario to explain how the double standard builds on itself to slow or even jeopardize a woman's career. Its subtlety lies in the fact that its effects are seen only when the toll has been cumulative.

Joe and Judy are each top M.B.A. graduates. A big plum assignment comes up. Charlie Managing Director has to choose between Judy and Joe. They're both stellar performers. But because they went to the same college or played the same sport, there's an intangible bonding between Charlie and Joe. And though it's hard to pinpoint why, Charlie's stronger affinity for Joe wins him the plum assignment.

Joe, no surprise, runs with the job and boom—gold mine! He performs. At the end of the year, Charlie does an assessment: "Joe, you did an extraordinary job on a challenging assignment. You delivered and we'll pay you for it. Judy, you did your usual wonderful job. Nothing real extraordinary this year, but we'll pay you this" (a figure significantly lower than Joe's).

Move into year two. Another assignment comes up similar to the one that Joe did. The managing directors say, "Should we give it to Joe?" Nobody stops to say, "Are we being managerially responsible with this decision?" Nobody is accountable for asking, "Is it time to give Judy this platform?" Instead, they give it to Joe again because the excuse is "We're short on time. We need this in six weeks so we need someone who's done this before."

Joe does the job. The rest is history. Joe develops a track record and his career takes off. Judy, if she wants to advance, will eventually get frustrated. She'll see herself in a go-nowhere mode. The managing directors will continue to give her more organizational tasks—the details and the OK deals but not the standouts.

Judy's one alternative for reparation is to speak up early and often: I deserve this. It's my time. Give me a chance. Unless she says that early on, the opportunity for redress will be gone by the time she raises it. And speaking up, if not done in just the right tone, will cause her to be labeled as "jealous," "frustrated," or "too aggressive."

Because she continues to give her all to her job, she may not even realize what has transpired until it's too late. The opportunity has passed. Judy's best option now is to go to another firm and maybe become a star, perhaps in a smaller arena.

The heart of this story is: Joe did a good job. No question about it. But Joe never had to ask for the opportunity. It's unfair, but Judy has to ask. If she doesn't, her fate is predictable: She will end up being great professionally but not fantastic. Joe will make managing director early. Judy will fall into that pool where senior management thinks "Well, she might make it," but it will take Judy five years longer than Joe. No one determines whether she didn't progress because she tried and failed or because she was never given the same opportunities as Joe.

Some who have heard this story conclude, "Sounds like whining to me." A closer look reveals a different explanation, complicated by the subtlety with which influence over careers is executed.

Bain & Company's Joanna Engelke describes the double standard's cumulative toll. "There are things that at the moment seem like no big deal except when you look at a career retrospectively. If you haven't done ABC this year, you won't be doing XYZ next year. If you haven't done XYZ next year, you're unlikely to be picked for the next opportunity. And I don't know if you can ever make up for those lost opportunities that build on one another."

THE GENDER LENS

Labeling people by gender alone can work both ways. Outside of Boston, about fifty women gathered for a meeting of the executive board for a local chapter of the Girl Scouts. After a talk on how to enhance the role models available to young girls, the sole man in the room raised his hand to comment. His response seemed to miss the session's point entirely and wandered off onto an unrelated topic. While his presence had been noted and verbally applauded earlier in the meeting, now he was a terrible disappointment. After the meeting closed, several women commented, "Boy, was he ever off base!" and "Weren't his remarks stupid!"

As the only man in the room, he, in effect, became the voice of every man. One reaction to his less-than-stellar remarks, reflecting the disappointment that the one and only man in attendance seemed unqualified for the group, might have been, "Let's never invite a man to our board again."

But perhaps the man was just tired or perhaps the women in the room could not relate to the point he was trying to make. Maybe he really was not qualified to contribute to the organization. Regardless of its origins, the women's disappointment conveys the closer scrutiny, and perhaps the higher standards, cast by the players—male or female—who control the situation and set the agenda for style and behavior.

Perceptions about style and expectations based on gender add yet another layer to the double standard for women. Sandra Bartlett* conveys a personal style that others have described as soft-spoken and polite. Senior managers have fallen into the habit of telling other women in the company whose style is more aggressive: "Why can't you be more like Sandra?" But Sandra finds this recommendation disturbing. "It's meant as a compliment to me—and my style has probably helped me to gain acceptance in the business community—but I find it troubling because it means that there is only one style acceptable for a woman. And if a woman comes across as aggressive and strong, somehow it's not well-received by male management."

Being viewed as aggressive can, frustratingly, damage a woman's career in professions where assertiveness and even combativeness are highly valued as traits in men. A 1995 report on women in large corporate law firms revealed stereotypes about business style that disqualify women from the same opportunities as men at their level. One is the assumption that women are less qualified for firm management than men, in part because most do not display the aggressive, combative style traditionally attached to lead attorneys. Another is the belief that women belong in client maintenance rather than client development because of the stereotype that men are better at networking and "glad-handing."[6]

Trial attorney Katherine Dresdner has been told that she is too aggressive in court. In the course of trying a recent case, the judge told Katherine that she was "beating up on the defendant" in her cross-examination. Katherine brought the court audiotapes back to her office where she asked her colleagues for their impressions. "I listened along with them. I didn't raise my voice on the tapes. I wasn't angry. I was just hard-hitting and wouldn't let the defendant avoid answering the questions. I pushed, but I never lost a basic calmness in the way I was doing it. No one in the office thought I had stepped over any kind of line." Most frustrating to Katherine is the double standard embedded in the judge's criticism. "When a man tries a case with the same style, the judge tells him he did a great job."

Despite an aggressive style and an extraordinarily strong track record, Katherine has found that female clients, more often than men, will interview her and ask, "Will you really fight for me?" The vast majority of her clients are, however, pleased with a style and expertise that wins their cases and also gives them personal support.

ARE WOMEN HELD TO A HIGHER STANDARD?

How much of the higher standard is self-imposed? And how much is imposed by workplace standards that favor men?

Wall Street's Marianne Bye comments, "I think there's this 'good girl' thing in us that makes us think we have to know everything before we take action. A guy can be more brazen. If he gets caught with his pants down, he just laughs and says, 'No big deal,' whereas a woman looks like an utter fool." Men can get by without knowing every detail on a project, but for a woman, the stakes are higher for not being absolutely prepared. "If you ever show any weakness in nuts-and-bolts knowledge, you really are never forgiven," observes Marianne.

Irena Makarushka, an associate professor of religion, agrees. "Women have to talk very succinctly, very cogently. I have heard men go on and on and say hardly anything worth hearing, and nobody interrupts them. For men, there's a higher tolerance for another man's incompetence than there is for a woman's."

Abigail Beutler, one of the early women managers at General Motors, now retired, believes that the higher standard renders ambitious women all the more threatening to many men. In her era, she says, the few women who made it to the executive ranks had credentials and skills far superior to most of their male colleagues. "The men seemed intimidated by our intelligence. They barely spoke to us."

Andrea Stevens,* a senior partner in a New York law firm, suggests that we can be our own worst enemies when it comes to setting a higher standard for women in the office. "All you have to do is to look at the three female partners. I hate to say this, but we're really terrible role models. All three of us are single. All three of us don't have children. All three of us have had to work harder to prove ourselves to the men."

ARE WOMEN HELD TO A DIFFERENT STANDARD?

Andrea Stevens tells other women that they need to get out from behind-the-scenes roles that slow down career acceleration.

Women often find themselves doing the administrative work that runs the firm while their male peers are out cutting deals on the golf course or over a drink. Andrea suggests, "I think to some extent we're more inclined to be good at the details. It's hard to get out from under the role of the detail worker, but as long as you are stuck in that role, you can't be very expansive and take on other functions." In her own firm, Andrea has found that even the women who are partners get called to draft the client papers, "but they won't call you to cut the deal."

Different tracking of men and women begins the day they walk through the law firm's doors. As Andrea explains, "It all comes down to the fact that men get exposure to the more important clients. They get included in the non-scutwork end of cutting deals and are more likely to be taken along to important meetings. They go to hockey and basketball games together so it's no surprise that they form a different type of relationship than with the women."

In her own career, Laurie Hawkes began to notice that the rules kept changing once she reached the level just below managing director. "Once, it was the year of 'Laurie, you did a great job. But it was the year of the star and you were only a team player.' The next year it was 'You were the star and this was the year of the team.' And the third year, they said, 'The department had a great year Laurie, but the firm didn't.'" They continued to affirm that she was on the managing director track, but there seemed to be a series of unfulfilled promises about the future.

The firm's real message, reflected in its abysmal promotion rates for women, confirmed its stubborn resistance to accepting women as key players. Laurie saw the handwriting on the wall and accepted a promotion to managing director at a competitor firm. In hindsight, Laurie would have moved to another firm sooner, but she was told the same story I heard from other women who are essentially talked out of leaving. When she asked about her future in the firm, top management offered what turned out to be unsubstantiated career assurance: "Laurie, you're vitally important to us. You must stay. We want you on our team."

Laurie has also noticed a difference in perceptions about, and, as a result, compensation for, women and men who make lateral moves. When men change positions within a firm, it's often seen as "he was so good in his last job, he should be able to fix this situation too, so let's give him a raise." For women who change departments the more common view is: "She's just started over. She doesn't know this area yet, so we can't really justify an increase."

Lynne Slater, an equal opportunity manager for the Goddard Space Flight Center, finds that women are held to a different management and work-style standard than men. "These women have had to be quite aggressive to get to where they are in a technical field. Their behavior is no different from their male peers, yet the prevailing attitude is that they shouldn't behave this way." And Lynne is certain that women often work harder than the men to overcome the gender barriers. One boss admitted to Lynne, "I wish I had all women working for me. You all work so hard." As Lynne points out, "Even if they do work harder, that doesn't always mean they're going to get ahead."

THE OLD BOYS' NETWORK

White, Male, and Worried," announced the headline of a 1994 cover story in *Business Week*, which described the white male's concern for the changing workplace demographics: "They recognize that they're still calling the shots and getting most of the promotions. But that does little to assuage fears that the pendulum will swing too far."[7]

Although women threaten men's long-standing workplace entitlements, the old boys' network remains a powerhouse behind the double standard. Ninety-seven percent of the women I surveyed believe the old boys' network perpetuates gender bias. Comfortable communication through informal socializing is one means by which the old boys' network is safely maintained. If you're not in the network, you're not on the inside track. This is the track that leads from the golf course and the locker room to a client's board, a high-profile project, or committee leadership.

For her male colleagues, Laurie Hawkes sees an open and welcoming path to this network. "They seem to be in the boss's office more often for informal chitchat. They are invited to hobnob with the bigwigs. I don't have time to do a lot of that, and I wouldn't be welcomed even if I did!" she says.

Men need to feel comfortable with women in order to accept them in senior management and on corporate boards. Fidelity Investments' Debbie Malins is convinced that "there is no way you'll get on a board unless the CEO and other board members are very comfortable with you as a player." Debbie watches with close interest how men use their comfort zone with one another to exclude women. "They trade favors. They really understand quid pro quo, but it's not necessarily anything that's blatant."

Women are often at a disadvantage when it comes to gaining access to the business networks from which clients are gleaned, but intrinsic ability is not the reason. In law firms, for instance, established clients who get handed down from retiring partners go to the men in the office, giving them a head start on a client base—a head start that the women partners don't get.[8]

MULTIPLE EXPECTATIONS

Among the women I surveyed, 88 percent view men's deep-seated discomfort with women's multiple roles as an obstacle to equal opportunity at work. Take Sandra Bartlett, for example. On a business trip to London, Sandra saw her role as a woman and her role as a woman in business collide. "As usual, it was me flying solo with the men and their wives," she recalls. (Sandra's husband had to conduct his own business back home.) When they arrived in London, the wife of a senior executive asked Sandra to take her shopping later in the day since she knew the city well. Sandra agreed, feeling that politically she really had no other choice.

Later that afternoon, one of Sandra's colleagues offered her a last-minute opportunity to meet a critical London player. But she couldn't make the meeting because, Sandra says, "I had promised to take someone on a *shopping* expedition—and she was waiting for me on a London street corner. It's sort of amusing now, but having a nonworking wife on the trip made the conflict between a working woman's multiple roles all too real for me." Whatever choice Sandra made would have put her in an awkward position professionally.

Nowhere is the double standard more apparent than on the work/family front. The man is a saint for staying home with a sick child. The woman is disorganized for not having back-up care. Janet Blake*, an insurance broker, has seen the double standard play out like this: "'Janet was late for this meeting. She was probably dropping her son off at day care.' But [there was] no mention of the other four men who walked in behind me. They must have been doing something important."

THE PROVING FACTOR

Janet Blake sees business development as another area where a woman is expected to prove herself again and again before she is finally welcomed to the inner business circles. "I've never been handed a business lead, although all my male colleagues have," she says, "so I bring in my own business. When I ask about a lead, they say, 'You're too busy.' But then I'm overloaded by having to both generate and maintain accounts. So my success is killing me." Janet has also noticed that her male peers "manage to scream and yell to get more support. If a guy gets too busy, they jump in to help him. For a woman, it's sink or swim on her own."

Men often walk through an office door with instant credibility. Lacking this advantage, women must find their own points of opportunity to build career momentum. Many women I spoke with used the phrase "I had to win them over before I could . . . ." The challenge for women who have no choice other than to build their own organizational credibility is not to let their confidence or morale sink in the process.

As Nancy Porter*, a high-tech purchasing manager, has discovered, "There are still very real biases and prejudices in the workplace, but I've been able to land on my feet because I know I can be valuable to the men there." Nancy got past the hurdles in an all-male division by passing the subtle tests through which men watched her performance. "I had to prove to them that I could speak their language. They threw every obscure acronym at me that they could. Then they wanted to see if I understood their technical requirements, so they would 'forget' to tell me one important specification. I had to make sure my information was 110 percent correct. That's how I won credibility."

Nancy has also found that outside vendors are more likely to challenge a written contract with her because she is a woman. When I asked Nancy for evidence of this double standard, she said, "I started tracking the vendors who tried to pass on a rate increase or renegotiate another aspect of the contract. It happens about 75 percent of the time. My male colleagues tell me they're only challenged by about 25 percent of the contracts."

Avoiding a Downward Spiral

What happens when a woman like the "Judy" described in Laurie Hawkes' story earlier in this chapter never gets promoted to managing director? If she doesn't specifically request developmental opportunities and succumbs to the predictable pattern set by the double standard, frustration can take over. And for some, this frustration begins to unravel one's effectiveness on the job. "All of a sudden," Laurie concludes, "she finds herself fulfilling the prophecy. The senior executives say, 'Judy's not much of a star. She just doesn't have it.'"

The daily detail work of marketing director Lisa Adams'* job became the catalyst for her new job search. At 29, she has just accepted a position in a small organization that seems to offer real career potential along with a 25 percent salary increase. In her last job, the operating rules were "If you want something done right, 'Give it to a woman.' The men can always slack off a bit."

At the job Lisa left, senior staff meetings regularly included discussion of how new employees were performing, including feedback from their customers. When Lisa suggested that a salesperson who had made a huge financial error should apologize directly to the customer, Lisa was greeted with "Look, he's a guy so he's not good at details. Women are good at paperwork and guys aren't." As Lisa looks back on this incident, she emphasizes, "Gender has nothing to do with my being organized. I just want to get the job done right."

A healthy team philosophy on paper does not ensure egalitarian rules in practice. As Lisa found, "My last company formed work groups so that it would operate more efficiently, but the groups were not really teams. The men played and won according to a different set of rules than the female team members." Seemingly small incidents, tells Lisa, were highly symbolic of the double standards for women and men.

When Jim, one of Lisa's peers, was assigned to her team for a major conference, "he only showed up for three of the fifteen meetings and never contributed anything—even though I had upped the sales—in a big way—for his last event," according to Lisa. The day of Lisa's national conference, Jim was scheduled to arrive for set-up at 8 a.m., but instead he strolled in at noon. While the firm's partners made a joke out of Jim's 4-hour delay, Lisa says, "If I ever did that! . . . And I never would. It's tempting, but I'm not one to blow off commitments." Lisa observes how easily a lower standard of responsibility gets passed on. "A new man was just hired right out of college. He sees what the other guys are doing so he follows in their path. They just laugh with him when he messes up."

Half of the women I surveyed believe that women are expected to take care of the office details while men are handed the plum assignments. Perhaps because of their ability to follow through on the more cumbersome management details, some women may find it easier not to delegate. And women who do delegate often find that it is harder for staff to accept delegation from them than it is from a man.

"Don't get stuck in the details. Never get too comfortable in a job." This is the advice many women pass on once they break into middle management. To position her career to keep moving forward, college administrator Mary McAteer Kennedy advises women to take the job nobody wants or is doing, but once you have mastered it, give it to someone on your staff. In her own case, Mary says, "When I first started in this job, I set up training programs. I love training employees, but I've delegated it to one of my managers now. Part of me hated to give it up because it's something I love doing. But it gives someone else a chance to grow into another set of skills and I can take on some new responsibilities."

Do Your Own Benchmarking

Professional association surveys and information in trade journal listings and current job ads can provide you with guidelines to fair and competitive compensation. Asking for feedback from your boss or from other trusted managers can help you determine options for advancement and can reveal how your career potential is perceived.

It's never too early to begin benchmarking on a job. When one vice president moved to a new division in her company, she decided she needed to counteract the "working-mom perception" that held her back in her previous position. Six months into her new job, she called her boss to say, "I've been here for half a year and I think this is a good opportunity to look back on what has occurred since I came on board." With a list of accomplishments in front of her and a copy for her boss, she set a standard for a conversation she would schedule again in another six months.

Each time she has been promoted, Mary McAteer Kennedy writes down the short-term, midrange, and long-term goals she has set for herself and for her department. Several times each year, she revises this career plan as she conducts reality checks to ensure that her professional goals align with the priorities for the organization. Mary has found two advantages to keeping her boss current on all news—both good and bad—in her department. For the positive outcomes, it helps her boss look good in the eyes of his peers. For the problem areas, Mary avoids, at all costs, the possibility of her boss being placed on the defensive without knowing the facts. "If you want your boss to back you up, make sure he knows what he's supposed to be backing you up on."

Joanna Engelke realizes that bosses are not always comfortable giving employees feedback and may be even less so with a woman. Perhaps they just aren't used to discussing business with women or perhaps they trade their normally direct style for a more evasive one, fearing a different response from women when they're given criticism.

To maximize her boss's comfort in giving her honest feedback, Joanna will say, "Would you mind if we take a few minutes and talk about—from your point of view—what went well in that presentation? Can we look at the role I played and how I can learn from this experience?" Joanna has found that bosses are more willing to talk with an approach "that doesn't feel like I'm asking them point-blank to criticize me."

To counteract exclusion from the career builders on which the old boys' network thrives, one insurance executive recommends, "Try to take the emotion out of emotionally charged issues." No manager wants to deal with someone who marches in and says, "I did all these things, so why aren't I recognized?" But your manager can respond with a straight answer if you say, "Tell me what it is I have to do to achieve the following goal. What kind of successes do I need to have behind me to take the next step?"

SUCCESSION PLANNING

Lynne Slater believes in information-based consciousness-raising to heighten the awareness of managers. Line managers, she believes, hold the potential to dramatically influence who advances in the organization. Knowing that she has the backing of top management in her equal opportunity manager position at the Goddard Space Flight Center, Lynne can call a manager to say, "You have twenty-three entry-level women in your organization who have gotten outstanding ratings at least three times in the last five years. What are your plans for them?" Lynne reads down her list name by name. "If they don't know who these people are, I encourage the manager to meet them. In six months, I'll go back and say, 'Did you meet so and so?' "

Carolynn Rockafellow, a managing director at First Boston Corporation, uses her established track record to pave the way for other promising women in the firm. Carolynn suggests that too often, the women who prove that they can perform "men's jobs" are considered the exceptions. The women in these jobs, she suggests, need to reach down into their organizations and encourage women at the next level down. They need to say in so many words, "This is how I got here. You can do this too."

Setting Your Own Standards

Joanna Engelke offers an optimistic perspective on counteracting the attitudes behind the double standard. "Every individual in a company can find a way to be effective, to make an impact, to change people's minds, to get things done."

To avoid the cumulative effect of the double standard, the women I met have figured out how to manage the expectations through which their ability and performance are judged. Their strategies can be used in any profession:

- Clarify your performance goals. Write them down. Confirm them with your boss. Do some benchmarking at regular intervals. And plan to exceed goals whenever you can.

- Ask for feedback from your boss, from team members, and from trusted colleagues.

- Adopt a political approach with your boss—problem-solving rather than accusatory—when you believe you missed out on an important career opportunity open to men with your same credentials.

- Ask the right questions—of your boss, of executive recruiters, of your professional contacts—to determine points of access to the next opportunity.

- Refuse to allow yourself to be limited to the caretaker-of-the-details function. Generate a plan for getting out from under general administrative work to clear the way for bigger contributions to your organization.

- Put your business contributions in writing with quarterly reports and spreadsheets that track the completion of projects and client updates. This documentation identifies your track record—often less visible than that of a man who has done the same work. When a salary increase or job upgrade is promised, confirm the timetable with a follow-up note to your boss. And begin planning how to keep your skills current.

- Recognize that there are times when the double standard is so deeply entrenched at the top and throughout an organization that your best option may be to move on to a job with a company whose corporate culture is more gender-blind.

- Don't give up on a style that works for you—even if it does not mirror the standards set by the way business has always been done.

CHAPTER 5

BREAKING THROUGH MIDDLE MANAGEMENT

"The reality is that our society hasn't really changed the rules of the game—it's only said: "OK girls, we'll let you try. But we're not going to change anything in the work culture."

—Cynthia Friend, chemist

Ninety-five percent of senior executives are men. Among this group, 97 percent are white men—a group that makes up just 43 percent of the workforce.[1] On corporate boards, women account for a scant 6.9 percent of the 11,700 corporate board directors.[2]

Why, with so many women in the managerial pipeline, aren't the numbers at the top higher by now?

A woman is readily accepted in the role of helper—a supporter of organizational functions bigger than her own—but for her to move past middle management, there must be a shift in the decision makers' views of her abilities and in their belief in her potential and commitment. Entering leadership positions requires a close, trusting relationship with peers and top management. The higher you rise in an organization, the more important are your relationships above and across your organization.

Between 1987 and 1991, the number of men in management increased by 3.5 percent while the number of women managers grew by 14 percent.[3] This increase for women, however, is not as encouraging as it seems at first glance. "If women continue to move into top business ranks at the current rate, the numbers of male and female senior managers will not be equal until the year 2470."[4]

Four hundred executive women surveyed by Korn/Ferry in 1992 reported that "being a woman" was their greatest obstacle to career success.[5] Similarly, a 1994 *Working Woman* survey of 502 female executives in traditional business organizations revealed their belief that the number one obstacle to women's advancement is "a male-dominated corporate culture."[6]

Eighty women of the 325 I surveyed identified themselves as senior managers. They include a CEO, a college president, managing directors in finance and consulting, senior partners in law and accounting firms, and executive vice presidents in banking and general management. They work in organizations ranging from a two-person operation to Fortune 1000 companies. Sixty-five percent are married; 60 percent have children. Senior managers were slightly more likely to have had a mentor than the women in middle and upper-middle management.

None of the women I met, even those at the top of their organizations, deny the existence of unequal treatment on the job. Among the senior managers, 62 percent believe the old boys' network perpetuates gender bias "to a great extent."

More than half perceive barriers to reaching their career goals, and the primary barriers are attitudinal and organizational, not personal. One woman in finance believes, "Subconsciously, my boss will never allow a woman to succeed him." A management consultant responded, "To keep advancing, I need to be more 'confrontational' rather than 'relational' and I don't want to adopt that style." And other women referred to some fundamental disadvantages in not being "one of the guys," such as "not being perceived as a power broker" and "being viewed as 'not committed' to my career when I have children."

My research shows that the women in senior management face the same gender barriers as those still moving up the management ranks. For example, the executive women are just as likely to experience language demeaning to women in their *current* position as are the women in middle and upper-middle management. And they are just as likely to view gender as a factor in limiting compensation, promotion rates, and access to clients.

Only in two areas do the women in the upper ranks indicate a significant difference of opinion from the rest of the sample. One, they are less likely to perceive gender as a factor in their ability to take risks. Thirty-seven percent believe that being a woman has limited their opportunities for risk-taking (versus 56 percent of the middle and upper-middle managers who feel that way). This difference can be explained by the fact that women further along the managerial pipeline are more likely to have the track record and institutional credibility to support a high-risk venture. And from a personal perspective, a woman who has already lived through the successes and failures associated with risk-taking may simply be more comfortable with taking chances on the job.

And two, nearly twice as many of the women in middle and upper-middle management believe that motherhood automatically means reduced career commitment. The executive women probably worry less about this labeling because they have already proven the skeptics wrong, consistently contributing to the business while raising their children.

By sheer force of their drive and determination, the women profiled in this chapter have begun to challenge career expectations that are based solely on gender and to recognize the gender traps, even if sometimes they cannot avoid them. Their strategies are based on a common premise: My abilities are not what will prevent me from entering senior management; the acceptance of women is. Now what can I do to clear a gender-blind path for my career?

The Gender Edge

Carole St. Mark's career profile speaks to gender obstacles that loom larger as a woman advances through middle management and beyond: acceptance and visibility. As CEO of Pitney Bowes

Business Services, she is one of the highest-paid women in the country. Carole offers both humor and a strong dose of reality in response to the question, "Have there been any turning points in your career so extreme that they could have either derailed you or made you mad enough to just push forward?" "Oh yeah!" she answered. "Practically every day!"

Being a senior woman in business is not *always* a disadvantage. Carole defines it as a blessing and a curse. "The good news is that you're highly visible and the bad news is that you're highly visible. You're noticed," she explains, "and if you do things well, you get a lot of publicity. I get calls to be on the boards of major companies all the time where I know my male colleagues don't. The bad news is that if I make a mistake, the whole world sees it. And when you mess up, as you sometimes do, the world can be pretty harsh."

For Carole, being "the first woman" has both accelerated her career and magnified gender barriers. One of her earlier experiences when she was at General Electric epitomizes the challenge she faced with each promotion into a job never before held by a woman. When she moved from marketing to personnel in the financial division, her boss took her aside and outlined her assignment. "Guess what? The chief financial officer hates you," her boss told her. "Now your job is to win him over." He did not mince any words in telling her that the CFO simply did not want a senior woman on his staff.

When Carole asked, "At least give me somebody who wants to talk to me," her boss insisted, "No, no. This is good for you. Go win him over." Carole looks back with an uproarious laugh at this early career trial, when the most welcome response she could expect from a male executive was, quite literally, a disinterested grunt. "In fact, for the first couple of meetings, the CFO could *only* grunt at me. He wouldn't even talk to me," she says. "So I just decided I would figure out his business needs, his biggest problems. And I would be the one to solve them."

When Carole started her career in 1966, she "assumed that people would be hostile to me—and they were. Every job I had was a position that a woman hadn't held before, so I expected that people would resist me—and they did!" Admittedly thick-skinned as an early trailblazer, Carole decided, "OK, this comes with the territory. I'll just have to work harder than anybody else. I always tried to figure out what I could do that would help whomever it was that resisted me. And it usually worked."

Carole's approach is typical of that used by many of the first women to reach the executive suite. One way to get there is to solve a tough business problem. Another is to work harder and longer than anyone else in the office.

What made a difference in Carole's career path were the bosses she was fortunate to have early in her career. These were men who focused on "How can the business benefit from Carole's extraordinary potential?" instead of "Should I go out on a limb and put a woman in this key job?"

THE STUBBORN BARRIERS

What is holding organizations back from recognizing the promise of thousands of women who are ready to contribute to bottom-line results but are currently underutilized by their organizations? In *The Leadership Challenge*, James Kouzes and Barry Posner suggest, "Innovation and change must be perceived as opportunities rather than threats if people are to feel strong and efficacious."[7]

Without a widely shared determination to transform attitudes about change—in this case, accepting women at the most senior levels—the opportunity for organizational reward remains widely unrealized. *The Managerial Woman*, written in 1976 by Margaret Hennig and Anne Jardim, offers an explanation for the middle management wall, which is still valid today. The men who support the organization's informal systems are "the insiders: people who understand and support each other, the structure, and the rules; people who share common aspirations and dreams; people who grew up with similar backgrounds; who played together, learned together, competed together . . . ."[8]

Insider status often grows tighter the higher up you move in an organization. As Hennig and Jardim conclude, "What makes this particularly threatening to the future of women in management is that the informal system is at the heart of the middle management function and grows still more critical with every step upward."[9]

When a top manager has to decide whom to promote among several qualified people, the choice often leans heavily toward someone known and trusted on a personal basis. At a certain level of competence, one might ask, What difference does the personal connection make if the individual promoted is qualified in the first place?

There are two problems with perpetuating the insider track. One is apparent: Consistent patterns of promoting men only may, as defined by the courts, constitute discrimination. The other is more subtle: Middle management marks a point at which performance standards become more subjective. Qualities such as leadership potential, decision making, team-building, and work ethic become important. And these qualities are evaluated through the gender lens of the insider, often narrowing the field of contenders for the next business opportunity.

Many of the long-standing rules of work, even if not by intention, exclude women's participation in the organization behind the organization: informal communication networks, access to job and client referrals, socializing with "the guys" after work. These are the forums where women are viewed as outsiders. They are also the systems through which managers and leaders are often identified.

Our Responsibility for Success

As women begin to change the informal systems that have shut them out, they have to confront their own expectations for career success. Are there any barriers that women may construct for themselves? The women I met are secure enough professionally to assume responsibility for the pitfalls we may unwittingly perpetuate for ourselves:

1. The "I am woman, therefore I am responsible for absolutely everything" trap.

By sheer force of habit, we can push ourselves into feeling as though we must resolve every problem in the office and take care of anything the rest of the team forgot to do.

Carole St. Mark has recognized this trap, even if she has not always been able to avoid it. While Carole feels a strong responsibility for each business decision she makes, she can also see the merit in being able to distance herself from unproductive blame. She carefully walks the sometimes delicate line between the trap of self-blame and the cop-out of "I can do no wrong no matter what."

When asked about barriers she perceives to reaching her career goals, Mary McAteer Kennedy, a college administrator in upper-middle management, replied, "Getting past the expectations—both personal and imposed—that I have to be the one responsible for everything at work and at home."

2. The caretaker-of-the-details trap.

A senior woman in banking described the catch-22 of being good at business details that, while admirable, can drain attention away from big picture issues and undermine the managerial role she has worked so hard to achieve. When a male member of her staff purposely neglected his responsibility for a client preparation, she almost fell into the trap of doing it herself. This banker now warns other women about failing to delegate effectively and then getting stuck in the mire of the small details. Admittedly, she says, it can be difficult to break the habit of automatically following through on cumbersome management details, which earlier in her career protected her credibility and helped her advance.

3. The "I must be the problem" pitfall.

For many first-generation executive women, the strategy for advancement—and even for survival—was to "fit in," not to make too many waves, and just work harder and longer than most of the men. Some chose to adhere closely to the male stereotype of the tough leader and inspired a new female stereotype of the "dragon lady" or the "queen bee." Undoubtedly, some of these early managerial women developed this hard-nosed approach as a way of surviving the hostility directed toward those who dared to be "the first."

To Conform or Not to Conform?

Like a well-trained sociologist keeping her subject at a safely analytic distance, Wall Street's Marianne Bye takes a remarkably objective view of each gender barrier she has faced. "Many aspects of bias are very subtle and almost imperceptible, but after awhile you begin to see some trends. And then it begins to seem real."

Marianne's career has thrived in the most macho of work environments: persuading investment bankers on Wall Street and businessmen in South America that she is a powerful enough analyst to swing investments into a deal. It has not always been an easy climb. Marianne has encountered situation after situation that has helped her to understand why some women evolve, by default, into the stereotype of the woman who is "touchy," "overly sensitive," who "doesn't have a sense of humor"—in short, the caricature of "the career bitch," the man-hating creature, machinelike in her production of good work but unliked by her male counterparts.

Within her own limits, Marianne has conformed to the male rules of the game as she maneuvers through internal office politics in the interest of building relationships so critical to her line of work. As she cautions, "It never, never pays to be a bitch. If you are bitchy or nasty, it will always come back and nail you." But Marianne is also realistic about the inherently competitive nature of her business that has nothing to do with gender and adds, "It never pays not to fight when you need to. And I am a fighter. But I also plan my timing very carefully and occasionally, I have had to resort to that 'bitch role.'"

Marianne's response to an Argentine businessman, who wasted no time in getting right to the point, saying "I do not work for a woman," was to view this as "kind of comical." She makes it a practice in such instances to say to her colleagues, "He's a foreigner so we'll give him a break." Putting professional ego aside, Marianne has had to allow less senior men to be her corporate mouthpiece in interacting with these types. Otherwise, she knows for certain that her South American clients would be so engrossed in thinking about how to get her off the podium that they would not hear a word of her presentation.

Although Marianne is confident that her analytical skills are at least as good as the men down the hall, gender has become a roadblock to closing high influence, multimillion-dollar deals. Regardless of how stellar her work is, Marianne sees clearly the barrier to the rainmaking deal before her. "By not being treated as an equal with my male counterparts, I am, in effect, less skilled in asserting my influence with potential investment-banking clients—who are themselves more readily persuaded by men." And physical image can play a role in the influence agenda. As Marianne explains, "It's not like I'm 6 feet tall with a husky voice. I'm 5'4", I'm blonde, and my voice doesn't boom."

CEO Carole St. Mark believes that a certain level of conformity need not imply weakness. "You have to know which battles to fight. I've always tried to conform as much as possible to the way the organization is—even if I don't like it. You've got to get along with people. I've never been strident. I think stridency—while you may get attention—turns people off," she says.

Chemist Cynthia Friend candidly admits that her early career strategy centered on conforming to the male codes of work conduct and on consciously developing a work ethic in which she consistently out-performed her male peers. "That was the pattern I developed—and I probably still follow it to some extent. But now, because I've been able to succeed playing by the rules, I'm in a position to change them."

As to labels attached to a woman who is assertive and ambitious, Cynthia advises, "Don't worry about being called a 'bitch.' That's basically just a tool men use against women to make them be good girls." She adds, "I'm not going to say you should be masculine all the time. In fact, it's better to rule with an iron fist in a velvet glove and not be concerned if you have to be aggressive once in a while."

Breaking Through a Closed Culture

Marianne Bye spends a lot of time with investment bankers who protect and isolate themselves in a tightly closed business culture. Rather than blaming herself for the difficulty of breaking into their circle, Marianne instead explains what creates *their* inability to deal with her. "They all dress alike. They look alike. They tend to hire people that look like them, and they play by very similar rules."

Exclusionary cultures like this breed contempt for anyone whose business style does not fit the mold. Marianne, at age 37, has to chuckle at the nervous signals the investment bankers still give her when she walks into a room; she reads them as an indication of their discomfort in opening up to others not like them. She observes, however, "how suddenly they relax when a tall guy or a man with gray hair comes in behind me as my alternate or teammate."

Marianne generously attributes certain aspects of this behavior to the fact that these men may feel they have no other option. "Probably the bankers are making the right choice—for the moment—when they bring in the older wise-looking guy." When they're running scared in a difficult economy, it seems less risky for them. But she does not think that this absolves her of her personal responsibility to accelerate the acceptance of women as deal makers and rainmakers.

On a daily basis, Marianne formulates a plan to increase the odds that, in spite of unfair or even hostile expectations about her performance, business colleagues will—without notice—find themselves focusing on her abilities. She uses this never-say-die attitude to refuel her own confidence, explaining, "If I lack confidence—even if I am perfectly comfortable with the work—it is going to come through in my delivery, in my performance."

More often than not, new clients assume that Marianne can never fully enter the closed investment business culture—until they see the high profitability in her stock profile. Recently, a company asked Marianne to "come in and give a talk to our middle managers and explain to them the industry trends. We need them to be aware of the new cutthroat competitiveness."

Walking into the brokerage firm's beautifully appointed wood panelled conference room, Marianne took note of the forty managers waiting to hear her presentation, said hello to one, dropped off a huge stack of handouts, and left the room for a few minutes. When Marianne returned to the room after making a telephone call to her office, she opened her presentation with pointed remarks about the industry's job security. "Each one of you should take a look to your right and to your left. Only one of the three of you will survive."

A year after her talk, Marianne heard feedback from the client that the managers were still discussing the session that "blew them away" with its hard-hitting look at today's fierce level of business competition. But, discouragingly, her client also told her that what made the biggest impact on the group members was their surprise that she came back into the room and was not "just a secretary" dropping off handouts. The assumption that she was not a manager would never happen to a man at her level in such a situation.

Identifying a Productive Niche

Women like Marianne have found ways to create success through innovative approaches and, in some cases, very high risk career strategies. By creating a novel, value-added product, professional recognition is eventually achieved.

Marianne used this strategy when she quickly seized an opportunity to educate herself on what she believed would become a sky-rocketing global telecommunications market. To make this decision, she relied heavily on input from her clients. What encouraged Marianne to learn a new market was that her clients themselves were faced with a new opportunity. "Sometimes opportunity comes at an unexpected time—and it is important to be aware of when to jump on it. When AT&T broke up, people from middle management were suddenly made CEOs of $15 billion organizations. When I started learning about the telecommunications industry, the whole sector started with new rules. This was my very first professional opportunity. Without a telecom background, I had to teach myself the industry." But Marianne had identified a career niche where everyone—regardless of gender— would begin at the same starting point.

WOMEN MANAGING MEN

Anne Clark*, a senior vice president in banking, faced an obstacle common to many women managers: How do you supervise a man who simply refuses to accept direction from a woman? When

Anne first became a manager, she inherited a staff she did not recruit herself, including Bill*, a younger and less experienced male colleague. After getting a lead on a promising client prospect, Anne handed Bill the complete business prospectus and said, "You ought to take a look at this. Analyze it. Then I want you to sit down with me and go over what you want to present. We'll go out and meet with this company in a few weeks."

A few days before the scheduled client meeting, Anne walked into Bill's office and said, "Why don't you take me through what you think the issues are." Barely looking up, Bill threw the prospectus across his desk and barked, "Can't you read it yourself!? I don't have any more time than you do."

"Bill, that's inappropriate," Anne responded. "I've given you a huge opportunity here. You need to pull this together before we see the client." But he never did. He could not answer the customer's detailed questions and failed to land the big account.

Anne knew that Bill had always cooperated with his male bosses, rather than pulling against them, so she decided to give him a second chance to "smarten up" and save his job. But she was well aware that her success as a new manager depended on taking a hard line with this man, whose personal hostility was a liability to the bottom line, and when Bill blew his second chance, Anne had no option but to fire him. She uses this incident, and several other less extreme ones, to assert the wisdom of effective delegation and decision making. Now she advises other women, "You have to reach a point where you set the tone, make your own rules, and establish limits on how much professional abuse you'll withstand."

The Solution to Sabotage

Effective management of people is key to any business career. And when those people are men and the manager is a woman, the stakes can be high indeed. When Carole St. Mark was first promoted to a vice president's position, more than a few men reacted negatively to what they considered the insult of working for a woman, not even making an attempt to mask their disdain toward her.

Even hard work, exceptional confidence, and stellar business results cannot guarantee acceptance of a smart, aggressive woman who is calling the shots. Carole frankly admits, "I have had a number of issues with some of the men who worked for me. They were company presidents so they had pretty big egos for the most part, and secondly, some held onto a real desire to do things their way and not tell me about it. And some had a *real* resistance to being managed by a woman." Much of their resistance was subtle—"forgetting" to tell her about important business transactions, talking about her behind her back—but some of it was blatant—overstepping the bounds of their authority and putting company funds at risk.

Like Anne Clark, Carole employs a direct strategy to remedy sabotage from members of her staff. "I have fired a fair number of male presidents because I get to a point where I have to say, 'You don't understand; I'm your boss. Goodbye.' And then they get it," she says. Carole carefully dots her "i's" and crosses her "t's" before she fires anyone, reviewing her reasons with the head of personnel and securing his or her concurrence. Over the last few years, she has fired two male presidents and explains, "I tend to give people a lot of rope. I don't address questioning of my authority as aggressively as maybe my male peers would—like beat them over the head with a baseball bat." she jokes. "But I don't allow them to take me for a fool either."

Five of the men who worked for Carole when she became a vice president were a generation older, and five others, she says, "were all these hotshot MBAs my age or younger." She went into her job assuming that the older men would be the ones to give her a hard time. The opposite became true. "Three or four months into the job, one of the older guys came into my office very early and was talking about the weather and shooting the breeze with me." As he walked out, he silently placed a piece of paper on Carole's desk and told her, "I think you should know about this."

That piece of paper revealed business plans one of Carole's subordinates was about to implement in direct contradiction to the business strategy Carole had articulated to her group. Carole later fired him for refusing, time after time, to follow her business objectives. And that, she concludes, finally got the attention of the other men who resisted her leadership.

TACKLING THE JOB NOBODY WANTS

For Carolynn Rockafellow, a managing director at First Boston Corporation, her thirteen years in investment banking have taught her one key career lesson: It is her principal business responsibility to analyze every decision in the context of how she can help the firm run better. In one instance, she designed a strategic plan that would eliminate her job, whose usefulness she knew the firm had outlived. As she explains, "My intentions are totally for the firm. They're not for Carolynn Rockafellow's betterment. The only reason I'm here is to be a partner—which is what I'm being paid for—to be the best partner I can with no political motivation."

Carolynn's most recent "ugly job" was to review and renegotiate every one of the firm's worldwide vendor relationships with a view toward reducing expenses by $50 million dollars a year. No one else would touch the job because it involved saying no to so many people. "Talk about how to become everyone's worst enemy!" she interjects, as she describes the less-than-pleasant responsibility of redefining corporate travel policy, monitoring the use of consultants, and tightening vendor selection. One dreary phone call after another—ranging from law firms to airlines—paid off in a reduction of $120 million in annual operating expenses. The job that nobody else wanted to touch paid off in rewards for the company—and for Carolynn's career.

The most successful business people are often those who have dared to take the high risk, which ultimately results in a big payoff to their organization. It involves putting personal ego to the side and preparing oneself for the possibility of stumbling in a big way. Carole St. Mark is one of these people. "I think the overriding strategy of my career has been to take the job with a big problem to be solved, one that can make a big difference in the business. I've always gone after those things that were tough, that maybe other people didn't want to do."

Carole's principal business strategy has been to focus exclusively and consistently on a few major business goals, tuning out skeptics and distractions around her. "I'm a *very, very* persistent person. I don't give up easily. If things don't go the way I'd planned, then I try a different way. I also work hard to develop allies, to convince people to come over to my way of thinking."

In 1980, Carole joined Pitney Bowes as director of human resources development. Advised by several trusted colleagues that the job amounted to "a suicide mission," Carole immediately accepted the challenge "because it seemed to be the one opportunity in my career when I could have a major impact on a major company." Coming from General Electric where executive assessment succession planning was done well, her mission at Pitney Bowes was to turn around a ten-year manager succession program that had never worked. Her predecessor had, in fact, quit out of frustration.

Facing words of discouragement at every turn, friends and colleagues warned Carole, "Don't take the job. It'll never work." That's exactly why Carole accepted the challenge. Her attitude was "Here's an impossible job. I'll take it!" Because the initial project had involved a huge amount of managerial time with no visible results, Pitney Bowes had become universally hostile to the concept of succession planning. Although the board backed the project, no real support existed. "The CEO at the time was 63 and even he hadn't chosen a successor," she says. "And he didn't want to."

Carole entered each job at Pitney Bowes with the clear mission of solving a big problem, knowing up front she would not be welcome because there had never been a woman at the company close to her level. Early on, she asked every senior officer in the company, "Tell me. Why don't you want to do succession planning?" Every one of them expressed extreme frustration that they had been put through a massive paper process, filling out "a zillion" forms and putting information into the company database, but nothing had come out of the process. Their challenge to Carole was "Good luck to you, but I'm not filling out one more form." Immediately, Carole heard a clear message from these officers—her internal customers—that whatever her process for succession planning, it had better be painless to them.

What was painless to the organization was downright grueling for Carole and the one person she hired. "For a year and a half, the two of us went around the world to interview the top 300 people in the company. We wrote skill assessments for each of them. Then we gave them back to the individuals and their bosses for their review. After that, we rewrote them."

In hindsight, Carole says, "I learned a lot. Even though it almost killed the two of us, everybody loved the process because they didn't have to do any work and still got this great output. That's how I got noticed by the man who became the new company chairman." The people who had at first been poised to watch Carole fail were there when the new chairman offered her a promotion to vice president for strategic planning.

Carole admits, "I didn't know anything about strategic planning then. And I was promoted over all these men who thought they were ready. Really, each one of them thought they should have gotten the job. And it went to this personnel person. And a woman. They were so insulted that I was made their boss."

Assessing that "these guys weren't going to help me," Carole set out to educate herself on strategic planning. To accelerate her learning curve, she at first sought the expertise of a consultant. Then she decided, "I'm just going to take a commonsense approach to this and cut through the process and do what seems logical to me. It wasn't the sophisticated process that the guys had been taught in business school, but it worked."

Again, analyzing why the in-place, long-range planning process had failed to meet the needs of its customers—in this case senior management—Carole took note of the thick piles of strategic plans gathering dust on bookshelves around the company. Then she moved into strategic action herself. "I changed the process completely to concentrate on the critical issues instead of volumes of analysis. I started a new approach that brought the key issues right to the surface, right to senior management—and then focused on 'What are we going to do about them?'"

High Risk and High Ambition

Carole's gutsy commonsense style paid off. One year after her first promotion at Pitney Bowes, she was promoted to vice president for corporate planning and development with prime oversight for new business development. Keeping her eye on the prize—profitable business outcomes—Carole tempered her tolerance for risk with confidence in her own common sense. "Because I was put in jobs where I didn't have the technical training—strategic planning, new business development, acquisitions—I just did what made sense to me. And that usually worked better than trying to apply a theory because I always kept in mind the result I wanted to achieve."

Although part of her job was to find new businesses for the company, Carole could not locate any acquisitions that looked attractive financially. So she started a new venture group inside the company. One new venture was based on the concept of an outsourcing business to run the mail rooms of other companies. At the time, she says, "We were selling a lot of mailing equipment. And our salespeople were telling us that customers were letting them know that mail rooms were not run well. There was a lot of staff turnover. So we thought, 'Hey, that's an idea for a new service.'"

By 1988, Carole's idea generated about $12 million in revenue. Soon after this, the CEO promoted Carole to president of business supplies and services. This was seen as an extremely controversial move. Carole admits, "I'd never run anything directly except the new venture, and he gave me a job that involved about a quarter of the company."

At this level, people were savvy enough not to make hostile comments in Carole's presence, but she heard through the grapevine people's resentment about "this staff woman who got this plum job to run a business." Carole herself stresses, "I admit I was not—on paper—qualified for the job. I'd never been a line manager, and here I was responsible for a $400 million business."

When I asked Carole, "But you knew you could do it, right?" she responded, "Oh, no. I didn't know I could do it! I *hoped* I could. I really didn't know." She said yes to such a high-stakes career move because, she admitted, "I was ambitious." Like many men who advance to the top of their organizations through a nontraditional track record, some career moves involve a leap of faith from a senior executive—and perhaps a leap of confidence from the one who's advancing.

High risk brought high reward. The CEO's shrewd appraisal of Carole's business talent proved absolutely on target. One of the initially small internal ventures she started is today the second-largest and fastest-growing business at Pitney Bowes—with 8,500 employees running mail and document-management centers all over the country. Now a CEO herself, Carole confidently reports, "I'm developing other new service businesses today. I love doing that!"

It's OK to Be Ambitious

Not every managerial woman follows the same model for work/life balance, but all of the senior managers I met are determined to follow the path that works for them. Debbie Malins, a senior vice president for Fidelity Investments, admits her perspective has changed since she recovered from cancer. "It used to be all career, but then I found I really needed to reassess which direction my life was going. I enjoy my job and want to do it well, but it's not my entire life. I keep it in perspective along with family, friends, and involvement in my community." Debbie, however, sees nothing wrong with fully immersing yourself in a job you love. "The key," she suggests, "is being comfortable with yourself and not worrying about what other people think. It makes life a lot easier."

Anne Pol was recently named to a list of 250 women most likely to be CEO. She readily admits that her lifestyle is nontraditional according to the conventional portrait of the guilt-ridden working mother. "At this level in corporate America," she says, "I don't think anybody can expect to have balance in their life. Men have to make sacrifices and women have to make sacrifices, too, if they are going to succeed in upper management. That may not be popular, but I really believe that's the case."

Married for twenty-eight years and the mother of a school-age daughter, Anne laughs at her own limitations in taking charge of household management. One recent evening, when she and her daughter made a stop at the supermarket, her daughter joked, "I'm going to have to go in with you because you don't know where anything is." Anne concedes, "She was right."

As president of shipping and weighing systems at Pitney Bowes, Anne leaves her house at 6:15 a.m. to work out at the gym for an hour and arrives at her desk by 8. Four nights a week, Anne leaves work at 8:15 p.m. to make the 40-minute trip to pick up her daughter at gymnastics practice, arriving home about 9:30 or 9:45. On Fridays, she gets home by 8:30 p.m. Anne seems to thrive on this grueling pace. And her family, she says, "happily doesn't know any different." The only time Anne has ever considered quitting her job was when the logistics for child care or after-school arrangements broke down.

On the subject of life balance, Anne replies, "I don't have any. The job wins all the time. The only thing I try to do is to save Saturdays and Sundays for my family. Unless the place is burning down around my ears, I try not to bring work home." Comfortable in her business skin, Anne speaks with a similar contentment about her personal life choices. "I used to worry about whether I was making the right life choices. Then I realized that I wouldn't be happy with an 8 to 5 job anyway." And she adds, "If I'm miserable, my family is going to feel it too."

LINE FUNCTIONS AND CREDIBILITY

Contrary to popular wisdom that pursuing a career in a traditionally "female" field dooms a career to second-tier status, both Anne Pol and Carole St. Mark rose through the ranks at Pitney Bowes via the human resource function. Even in human resources, which often becomes a staff function bogged down in paperwork and bureaucratic compliance issues, each sought out line positions and visible, sometimes risky, initiatives. This kept them moving through the managerial pipeline.

Anne, a former junior high teacher, quite deliberately established a track record in line jobs with the specific aim of building credibility and "getting over the gender issue." If you've always been in a staff job, says Anne, then the operating people don't feel that you understand what they really do on the job. Line jobs, she found, fostered organizational confidence in her ability to produce tangible business results.

In the eleven years she has been at Pitney Bowes, Anne has held six different jobs, making lateral and even sublateral moves but always apprising senior managers of her interest in learning new areas of the business.

CHOOSING WHICH BATTLES TO FIGHT

In the interest of funneling all of their time and energy into big-picture business issues, the new managerial woman has learned to let go of many career frustrations that only a woman faces. Confident enough to identify and to ask the tough business questions, she simply tunes out men who question her abilities on gender alone. As Carole St. Mark suggests, "It's not a good idea to fight battles that are purely personal. It quickly becomes clear to people that you're fighting for your own ego. The battles ought to be fought for the good of the company. Not that you shouldn't fight for your position—you should. But I think the egocentricity of a lot of senior people gets in their way and takes people down faster than anything else."

Cynthia Friend, a top-flight scientist, cautions women against letting the cumulative toll of a hostile environment derail their careers. "I know quite a few women who have a tendency to focus on the minor issues more than they should and that distracts them from their primary goal. It makes them less effective on important issues. You need to choose where you will take a stand and how you will do it."

Now that Cynthia has achieved tenure in an almost exclusively male field, she can use her position as a platform for change on issues she believes in passionately: flexible career tracks, family leave policies, work standards that allow a personal life. She firmly believes that one person *can* make a difference, and reports from her own experience, "Once you have achieved some level of success, people *will* listen to your viewpoint."

THE RAINMAKER AGENDA

Kathleen Ragot, a CPA, has noticed a radical change in this new generation of women business leaders. "Until recently," she observes, "if you looked at the women who succeeded, you'd see that they behaved much like the men. They were hard chargers—'Let's see how many overtime hours we can clock.' And even in the way they spoke, they were tough and purposely masculine." Kathleen never viewed these women as role models. But today she is encouraged by a new style of senior woman and quickly points to the example of a partner who shows her human side. "Her style is a bit more relaxed than the typical senior manager. She talks about her family and isn't afraid to say, 'I'm going to get this done right away so I can be home with my kids.' I respect her more because she's not just a work machine."

While there is no one portrait of the new managerial woman who's moving toward the top, certain common themes emerge from their individual career stories:

- All are supremely confident business strategists. They have gained the respect of peers and colleagues by mastering a style both comfortable for them and effective for their organizations.

- Women at the top, or on a rung close to it, exhibit determination that is unshakable. All have paid their dues in grueling hours and in some truly miserable job assignments, but on the vast majority of mornings, each looks forward to heading into her office.

- They tackle and solve the big problems. None backs away from assuming risk on the job. Adept at determining which battles to fight and skillful at educating themselves on the unwritten rules of their organization, none hesitates to make tough decisions in the best interests of their company. As Carole St. Mark suggests, "Take on the hard problems. Then you've got to be willing to really suffer through them. But if you can solve a hard problem, you've got it made."

- They hold a vision for success. All convey a strong results orientation bolstered by a crystal-clear view of their own business worth. Putting personal ego aside, their careers succeed because they define their on-the-job issues in the context of meeting the best interests of the business. And they work diligently to develop alliances that will support these interests.

- Early, as opposed to later, in their careers, they strategically carve out a niche where their business value will be apparent.

- Guilt is not a part of their vocabulary, either professionally or personally. Occasional self-deprecation is permitted. Self-blame, if it limits potential, is not allowed.

- They exhibit a focused understanding of the behind-the-scene rules of work that determine how their business is conducted. Clear career goals, coupled with a fierce determination to succeed, keep them from being discouraged by the barriers that persist for women at work.

- These women have, in the most macho of fields, made it to the top while helping others along the way. All take serious responsibility for identifying and supporting other women and for working to change the rules of work that held them back.

- They believe in themselves. Women like Marianne Bye on Wall Street and Carole St. Mark at Pitney Bowes have learned not to get bogged down in the eccentricities of corporate life. They refuse to allow the traditional male codes of conduct to slow their careers.

CHAPTER 6

RESOLVING THE HARASSMENT DILEMMA

"At 19, I was shocked and silent when I encountered harassment. When I was 28, I was discouraged by it. At 37, I take it for granted and tell the man that his wife and daughter wouldn't appreciate his behavior."

—A government officer in upper-middle management

The 1990s marked four pivotal milestones in sexual harassment case history. One of these, the multimillion-dollar settlement by the Baker & McKenzie law firm, set off a brief—disturbingly brief—wave of panic in boardrooms across the country as executives discussed how to avoid suits of their own.

The $3.5-million punitive damages award to a former employee at Baker & McKenzie, the country's largest law firm, ignited a firestorm of interest in what constitutes a "hostile work environment" for women. This was the case in which a firm's toleration of a partner's behavior, widely known for harassing office staff, brought charges not only against the offender but against the firm as well.

The shock of the magnitude of this award should have been a wake-up call to American business, but it was not. Ideally, it should have caused enough concern to direct every business—from small start-up venture to giant corporation—to get serious about changing work environments that are hostile toward women.

Before Baker & McKenzie, in 1991, the country had watched Anita Hill face off in a "he said/she said" battle against Supreme Court nominee Clarence Thomas and members of the United States Senate. In that same year, Stanford neurosurgeon Frances Conley put her job on the line to take a stand against the deeply entrenched and unchallenged locker-room mentality common to her profession.

Next came the Navy Tailhook scandal where whistle-blower Paula Coughlin's career suffered more than her harassers'. The Tailhook scandal exposed the profoundly serious defect in passive tolerance of a "boys will be boys" mentality, readily excused by the high stress of flight careers. For Paula Coughlin, speaking out immediately after the harassment occurred should have brought resolution to behavior that had been tolerated for years, but somehow she became labeled as the troublemaker.

For Anita Hill, just the opposite was true. Not speaking out sooner weakened the credibility of her compelling testimony. Regardless of whether she or Clarence Thomas told the truth, Hill was doomed to fail, in part because she did not terminate her employment with Thomas immediately after the alleged harassment occurred. The intense public scrutiny imposed on both Anita Hill and Paula Coughlin speaks vividly to the question: If so many women experience harassment, why do so few speak out?

According to the 1990 Equal Employment Opportunity Commission (EEOC) guidelines, sexual harassment is defined as follows:

Unwelcome sexual advances, requests for sexual favors, and other verbal and physical conduct of a sexual nature will constitute sexual harassment when: 1. Submission to such conduct is made either explicitly or implicitly a term or condition of a person's employment; 2. Submission to or rejection of such conduct by an individual is used as the basis for academic or employment decisions affecting that individual; or 3. Such conduct has the purpose or effect of unreasonably interfering with an individual's academic or work performance or creating an intimidating, hostile or offensive academic or work environment.

No one really knows how many women are harassed at work each day. Fear of reprisal and even concern about losing their jobs hold many women back from reporting sexual harassment. Anita Hill's testimony appeared to give many other women the courage to speak out about their own experiences: Between 1991 and 1993, harassment complaints filed with the EEOC nearly doubled—from 6,892 in 1991 to 12,537 in 1993.[1] But evidence is strong that most harassment goes unreported.

Fifty percent of the women in my sample of 325 have experienced harassment according to the EEOC definition. Many indicated that they have been harassed more than once. Eighty-five percent of the time, they handled the incident privately with the offending individual, largely due to the stigma attached to those who file complaints. Thirty percent of the time, they reported the incident. Offenders were most likely to be superiors, followed by clients, and then peers.

Since language, from a legal standpoint, constitutes one of the "gray" areas in the definition of harassment, I asked the women in my survey a separate question about whether they had experienced language demeaning to women in their current position. Sixty-nine percent responded that they had, some on a daily basis and others less frequently. My findings are similar to those of a 1992 Korn/Ferry survey of 439 women executives in which 59 percent reported that they had experienced sexual harassment at work, but only 14 percent reported it.[2] Many women suffer in silence.

Some of those senior enough to have less concern about job security confront their harassers privately and directly. Some extricate themselves from difficult situations by changing jobs while claiming other reasons for their move.

Mary Rowe, ombudsperson at the Massachusetts Institute of Technology (MIT) and a pioneer in strategies to remedy all forms of harassment, estimates that of the 6,000 concerns about harassment she heard over a sixteen-year period at MIT—from inside and outside the institution—at least 75 percent of those affected worried about negative consequences for bringing forward charges: job reprisal, social rejection, peer and family disapproval, loss of goodwill, and, in some cases, violence.[3]

In any work setting, the unwritten rules place an extraordinarily high value on "goodwill"—getting along with the team, avoiding behavior that appears disloyal, keeping the peace between coworkers. Being labeled a troublemaker can mean quiet death for a career. The fallout for bringing forward an allegation of sexual harassment can be destructive to a woman's career from several angles: when the woman's name is not considered for committee leadership, when the invitations stop for the important client dinners, when she is silently excluded from informal office exchanges. She, rather than the harasser, becomes the outcast in her organization. What can a woman do to counteract the indignity of being forced, for fear of reprisal, to suffer in silence?

Even when the harassment line is definitively crossed, women fear career reprisal for going public with an allegation. Yet they also worry about personal integrity for taking no action at all. As a woman who manages a large, male-dominated staff explains, "Passively accepting harassment would diminish my authority."

To remedy a situation that involved wolf whistles and sexual innuendo every time she walked past a colleague, she spoke to the offender directly. When it became apparent that the meaning of her words had not sunk in, she called a meeting with both the harasser and his boss. She made it clear that she would not report the harasser if, and only if, the offensive behavior stopped immediately. "I didn't want him to lose his job; I just wanted the harassment to stop." And it did. She may, in fact, have saved the person's job since soon after the harassment stopped, the president of her organization issued a firm directive on zero tolerance for sexual harassment.

Does a woman sacrifice her integrity when she chooses this approach? No, say many of the women I met, not if your intention is to stop the harassment and keep your career moving.

A new, perhaps more political and realistic attitude prevails among courageous women who are helping to set new standards for what is acceptable and what is not for workplace behavior. They are, one by one, putting a stop to behavior that makes the workplace a battle zone for women—without having to go to court.

Formal complaints and litigation are not the answer for the vast majority of women who have suffered harassment. It's expensive. It's time consuming. And even if a woman wins her harassment case, her career is the likely loser. The threat of litigation has done little to change corporate behavior. It has only pushed it underground a bit.

MUST BOYS BE BOYS?

Law partner Catherine Lee describes a common form of harassment experienced by many of the women in my survey. As Catherine explains, "I've put up with being called 'honey' and 'sweetie' for years. I bit my tongue when a major client prospect commented on my legs. But the day a European client called me 'pussycat' (after weeks and weeks of 'sweetheart') I drew the line. That was more than I was prepared to take from anyone." Catherine immediately told the client, "I do not want to be called pussycat. In fact," she added in a lighter tone, "in this country, people can go to jail when they make persistent and unwanted comments like that." Her client, at first, laughed, but then, says Catherine, "He woke up and got the point for the rest of the time I represented him.

Catherine feels a responsibility to stop harassment in a way that will, if possible, educate the offender. She has changed her strategy as she has moved up the ranks and explains, "The challenge is to try to say something that will be understood, that will be heard—as opposed to earlier in my career when I was less confident and less secure in my position and I felt more angry." As is the case for many women, the anger and frustration that come with being harassed have a great deal to do with not having the power to stop it.

An episode of the television show *Grace Under Fire* portrayed a too easy, yet commonly accepted, rationale for "boys will be boys" behavior: the majority rules, defend-the-pack excuse. When challenged about his tolerance for demeaning and sexist comments, one oil-refinery manager counters, "What am I supposed to do—tell nineteen productive workers to change or tell one worker to get with the team? Grace, that's not harassment," he argues, "that's math."

94

The price for becoming one of the boys can exact a terrible toll on a woman's business credibility in the long-term. Susan Cohen's* story points to the danger in accepting, tolerating, and even imitating the machismo of male colleagues. To conduct business with a young, primarily male Wall Street crowd, Susan thought she could gain acceptance as "one of the guys" by following their lead in heavy drinking and using crude language. When she decided she needed to work under higher standards, none of her colleagues took her seriously. Susan now offers a stern warning to her younger female colleagues. "Once you accept their behavior, once you go along to a 'girlie' show because you think you have no other choice, you live with these standards forever."

Some men who harass women rely on the safety-in-numbers theory to protect their standards of behavior. The long-standing explanation that men just don't know better, that much sexism is inadvertent can become too easy an excuse. On the other hand, as harassment expert Mary Rowe notes, "The more I learn about race and ethnicity as a white person, the more I understand the point of view about how ignorance leads to offense. I have myself once offered food to somebody with my left hand, not realizing that to that Muslim this was a very insulting gesture. It is easy to be misunderstood ethnically, racially, sexually."

Despite the possibility of misunderstanding certain kinds of comments or actions, most harassment is painfully clear in its intent. Taken individually, comments like "Let's invite her to the meeting; she's easy on the eyes," or "What's the matter? Got PMS today?" seem unworthy of response or attention. Experienced cumulatively—at the coffee machine, after a client presentation, on the way into an important meeting—they demean a woman's business talent and undermine a fair chance at professional respect. The long-term impact is wearing and demeaning.

FINDING RESOLUTION RIGHT FOR YOU

For Caryn Moir, harassment began with irritating comments from the man in the next office: "Would you like to go to Tahiti with me?" "Would you marry a man who'd been married three times?"

Caryn, known for her confident, no-nonsense style, would answer with characteristic humor, "I wouldn't even date a man who had been married three times." When the harassment turned perverted, Caryn's humor and patience with her offensive colleague began to wane. Pregnant with her first child, she began to receive pornographic videotapes in the mail—on her birthday, on holidays.

Physically sick from a difficult pregnancy, Caryn understandably could not find the energy to file a formal grievance, but she wanted her harasser to know that she was "on to him." Caryn recalls how she felt when she finally confronted him. "I was eight months pregnant and big as a house. I felt like a tank—being 60 pounds heavier. And we had lost our cat the night before; he'd gotten hit by a car." And this was the morning the harasser chose to make nasty comments about Caryn's membership in the company's women's organization. Thinking more about the videotapes than his insults that morning, Caryn says, "Finally, I told him, 'Back off!'" His verbal harassment stopped, but the tapes began to arrive with greater frequency.

"I didn't want everyone to think I was a crybaby," explains Caryn. "All my life I've heard that if you want to be successful in business, 'Don't go whining about stuff you can handle yourself.'" But after nearly a year of regular deliveries of X-rated films, Caryn worried that she might need some sort of protection in case the harassment got even worse. She quickly learned that even when a company's official policy denounces harassment, the burden to prove and document the case falls on the woman herself. "In those early days when I was handling the harasser myself, I needed to document every conversation. Well, we all know how busy our lives are—and I have to write down every snaky comment he makes to me?! I don't think so." As Caryn points out, even in a company that offers full support in resolving harassment, much of the burden of proof falls on the victim.

A woman may begin to feel that the harasser is controlling her life in a different way when she begins the often-frustrating process of documenting his actions. As Caryn suggests, "It's difficult to think about going through some kind of legal action while I'm working in an environment where I'm supposed to be a team player. Also, I may have to implicate people who may not want to get involved. There's a lot of 'Whatever you do, don't involve me!' And I have to continue to work in this environment."

Caryn admits, "Confronting harassment becomes extremely personal. For me, it was frightening for awhile, thinking that this guy might come after me. It was something that almost struck fear in me." Fear, becoming "prey" to a harasser, becomes another form of a harasser's potentially destructive power.

Despite conflicting emotions about what course she should follow, Caryn says, "I finally made it really loud and clear in the office that I had been receiving these tapes. I made it obvious that I was going to prosecute and made comments about getting fingerprints." Soon after this, the harasser left the company.

What is instructional about Caryn's case is not so much the disgusting nature of the harassment she experienced but the fact that her first concern was about being perceived as an oversensitive, whining female if she pursued a formal investigation. "Everybody agreed that I was being so cooperative," she says. "They thought I was being mature and 'a big girl.' The kind of feeling I got was 'Boy, you're being such a good sport about all this.'" Women like Caryn recognize that they are often scrutinized closely for how they handle these extremely delicate situations even in the context of an open and supportive work culture. And, Caryn adds, "I love working for Pacific Bell. I would not stay here if this were not a healthy environment."

If a woman like Caryn, who works in a company committed to resolving sexual harassment, was reluctant to speak out about this egregious version, it comes as no surprise that most women choose not to go public about the more common, if less extreme, forms of harassment. Caryn's story also explains why women need to choose a course of action that is absolutely comfortable for them.

What do the experts on resolving the harassment dilemma advise? Even they do not always agree on what is the best course of action. Lynne Slater, equal opportunity manager for the Goddard Space Flight Center, suggests that choosing an effective remedy depends on the individual situation as well as the style and temperament of the person being harassed. "Some women are strong enough to just go to the guy and say, 'Look, buzz off!' A lot of women are not. But if they are, I think that's the best way to go." The ability to take such a direct approach is highly dependent on the strength, or perceived strength, of a woman's professional position. A woman with a long track record and a supportive boss is in a much better position to speak up than a woman who has not been part of a company long enough to build political alliances and a solid professional reputation.

Because every employee at the Goddard Space Flight Center has received training on sexual harassment, Lynne Slater can, in good conscience, recommend warning a harasser directly or asking a boss to intervene "so there's a common language," she says. "The managers and staff know what the game plan is." Although Lynne admits that not every manager is entirely comfortable with her approach, everyone in the organization has been given the opportunity to understand what is acceptable behavior and what is not. And Lynne knows that top management supports her position.

Even in an organization like the Goddard Space Flight Center, where employees are well-educated and there are clear procedures for anyone who is harassed, women still fear reprisal for speaking out about harassment. Women have relayed to Lynne again and again observations that point to the insignificance with which many managers regard the issue. For example, she often hears comments like "I mentioned the harassment to my boss and he handled it, but he thought I was stupid for not just ignoring it." And the perception that a woman is "stupid" or oversensitive will influence whether or not her boss considers her for assignments and growth opportunities.

And what if the harasser is someone who can hold your job security or the completion of an important project over your head? The "Now look creep, this can't go on" strategy may not be a wise course if the offender is your boss or someone who can have an impact on your paycheck or career movement. When the offender is someone's immediate supervisor, Lynne brings the case to the supervisor's boss. When it is an outside contractor who is doing the harassing, Lynne asks the internal contracting officer to call the harasser directly and put pressure on him to "clean up his behavior." Their consistent message is "These are the rules you will work under. If you cannot, we will terminate the contract." The message is simple and straightforward. And the word gets out to other contractors. As Lynne adds, "That's one thing that I don't mind leaking out."

A WHISTLE-BLOWER'S COURAGE

In 1991, Frances Conley, M.D., decided that expecting women to handle the humiliating experiences she encountered every step of the way from graduate school to the top of her profession was too steep a price to pay for someone whose profession is life-saving surgery. By virtue of her unusually high organizational value as one of a tiny number of female neurosurgeons nationwide, Dr. Conley took the calculated and courageous risk of resigning from her job to protest the promotion of a known harasser.

At the time she resigned, Frances was chair of the medical faculty senate at Stanford and had just been elected to a prestigious University committee. She was also running an internationally known research program. So, she says, "It was obvious to everybody that I was not crazy." Just why did she resign? Because a man widely known for his consistently demeaning language to women, including Frances, was appointed department chair. She could no longer tolerate his behavior in the hallway, in meetings, and in other public settings, where he would yell comments such as "You're being difficult today. You must have PMS," or "You're not being a team player. You must be 'on the rag.'" Frances knew that other women had filed sexual harassment charges against this surgeon, but they had basically been ignored.

Frances made her point. A committee investigated the allegations against the surgeon, and, after demoting him, they asked Frances to return to her professorship in neurosurgery. She did. Frances was able to take courageous action because, as she explains, "I was dealing from a hand of tremendous strength. I have tenure. I'm a full professor." But even for a woman with her professional clout, courage has come at a price. "I am persona non grata at Stanford and will not go any further in deanships or medical administration."

Overall, however, Frances knows she did what she needed to do and has received more than a thousand letters of support confirming that opinion.

Frances advises other women to "take a good look at the pluses and minuses before you act. And if the minuses outweigh the pluses in terms of the career you would like to have, then you had better swallow hard. Try to diffuse the harassment in any way you can, but start documenting what's happening right at the start until you have a critical mass of facts. Then you have the evidence if you decide to make your move."

The Gray Area

Should we feel any sympathy for the man who says, "All this talk about what I can and cannot do is making me paranoid. I'm afraid to even talk to the women in my office"? Is it harassment when a man compliments a woman on her new suit? Certainly not, if his behavior is consistently professional in all respects. But yes, it could constitute harassment if the comment follows a series of her refusals to the question, "Won't you come to my beach house this weekend?"

Most reasonable people have good instincts about what constitutes demeaning, offensive, and harassing behavior. Many women decide that they will take a higher road than that chosen by their harasser. As MIT's Mary Rowe notes, "I do feel a social obligation to allow anyone who isn't a truly awful person to save face." A natural and understandable reflex to a demeaning incident is an angry retort or a stern lecture. When the purpose is both to stop the behavior and to avoid career reprisal, some women decide to allow the offender to save face: "If this a social invitation, I'm very honored, but I won't be able to come." No emotion, no explanation needed.

Even the best definition of what constitutes a hostile work environment is highly situation-dependent. As Mary Rowe suggests, "Harassment is an unusual 'wrong': It exists in part in the eye of the person wronged rather than having a wholly objective life of its own. For example, sexual harassment is legally defined in part as being unwanted sexual attention." [4]

Mary describes the difficulty in clarifying where poor judgment ends and harassment begins. "There isn't a clear line except as defined by each person. Imagine, for instance, somebody who has been abused in childhood. She may need a workplace that has no images in it that recall gender to her. And conversely, somebody brought up as the only sister among eleven brothers—who was the best football player among them—may have no problems at all with raunchy chitchat."

Difficulty in definition does not excuse the need for resolution of a troubling, if often secret, workplace dilemma. How can managers set standards that are equitable and fair while covering a broad spectrum for individual levels of tolerance? How does a woman define for herself where her own lines of tolerance will be drawn?

Caryn Moir hesitated at first to take action against an extreme form of harassment largely because she was concerned that confronting the offender would do more harm to her career and her state of mind than the harassment itself. And if the stakes seem this high for the outrageous behavior that Caryn faced, dealing with the "gray" areas of harassment are all the more difficult. Women who "cry wolf" do all women a disservice. Caryn knows a woman "who knee jerks to every comment and is threatened by everything. Nobody pays attention to her after awhile, and she makes it harder for other women to speak out."

The best way to handle a hostile situation depends on how a woman evaluates the intent of the offender: Is his behavior simply poor judgment? A generational gap? Or does he know better? Is he just busting my chops? Karen Hoyt*, an executive in a manufacturing firm, suggests, "There are things I will say to some people that I wouldn't dare say to somebody else. You have to take the pulse of the situation, and you certainly don't want to do anything that will publicly embarrass the other person, regardless of what he's done to you, because then you're on his list forever."

Trying to classify language as either offensive or hostile or showing poor judgment often means walking a delicate line. At a company conference, Karen was approached by a vice president who greeted her with a "Hi, sweetheart, how are you doing?" She replied with a "Well, hi, poopsie, I'm fine. How are you?" After a brief look of amazement, Karen says, "He just gave me a big smile and walked away. I had done this jokingly so he knew I wasn't being malicious—but I was making a point about respectful language."

Karen bristles when she thinks of other situations—like business social gatherings and professional conferences—where women are expected to tolerate a different standard for physical contact. Frequently at such events, she extends her hand, intending to shake hands with a male colleague who instead puts his arm around her and plants a kiss on her cheek. "That just blows my mind," she says, "because I don't even know these people well. I don't like people touching me and I certainly don't want them kissing me unless they're a really close friend. And even for a friend, I wouldn't expect them to kiss me in a business setting." These are the situations where women find extrication difficult and embarrassing. As Karen concludes, "In these cases, I just get out quick and don't go near the person again. You can't make this an issue when you're in the middle of a group of people. Not if you want to survive."

SEXUAL HARASSMENT'S LONG-TERM MEMORY

As women described their experience with sexual harassment, many talked of never having told anyone—not even a friend or family member—about the incident. They have learned to hide the human toll of the embarrassment and shame they feel—for something over which they had no control. One woman, now in a corner executive office, recalls an early point in her career when harassment was not widely recognized. "We were at an off-site conference. I was walking to my car and I noticed an older man whose car was far away, so I said, 'Do you want a ride?' And he said, 'Sure.' He got in my car and immediately grabbed me and kissed me. And I was just horrified. It was the last thing in the world I expected. I was very upset about it. I didn't know what to do so I told no one."

The real import of harassment is not in how it is defined but in what it does to the person who experiences it. Regardless of the specific circumstances, harassment is disturbing, demeaning, embarrassing, annoying, and frustrating. Women who've been sexually harassed carry the heavy burden of wondering whether they should have said something to the harasser, whether they did anything to cause the incident, why they were unable to take action that might prevent the next woman from being harassed.

Karen Hoyt* still carries the vivid memory of the explicitly drawn nude woman that greeted her the first day she entered the executive dining room. "In my wildest imagination, this was not something I expected." As the only woman among forty male managers, Karen nervously sat down at one of the two tables reserved for executives. "All of a sudden, the lazy Susan stops in front of me, and there's a white sheet of paper on which someone has drawn a naked woman, spread-eagle. Nothing is left to the imagination. And I'm thinking, 'Gee, do I make an issue out of this? Do I react? What are they waiting for?'" Karen decided not to say a word. After a few more spins around the table, an older male noticed the drawing and said, "This is terrible," as he removed it from the table.

Sitting at this lunch, Karen recalled the advice she had heard from Carole St. Mark, then a vice president at Pitney Bowes, who spoke at a Simmons College management course. "Choose your battles very carefully. You can't win them all." Karen had made the political decision not to give in to the emotional reaction the group at her table expected from her. "I decided this was really petty and childish and that I didn't want to get involved in it. They were looking for me to get upset, so they could say, 'See, we told you she wouldn't be able to handle this job.'" And, she adds, her decision was probably a wise one. "One of those guys ended up being my boss a couple of years later."

Even if simmering hostility toward managerial women does not turn destructive, it can cause these women to question their personal integrity and can undermine their professional confidence. Although Karen has never before spoken about this incident, she now reflects, "I've never forgotten that. It left such an indelible mark in my brain. I will remember it forever. And it really does something to you because every time I see one of those guys, I wonder, 'What did they think of me as a person that would make them do something like that? Just what were they trying to tell me?'"

Over the years, Karen has maintained her cool in a variety of other hostile encounters with her male peers and colleagues. When asked whether this first less-than-welcoming experience fortified her for other challenges, Karen replied, "I now know that I can rise above that kind of behavior. I don't need to deal on their level. It wouldn't serve any purpose."

THE CLOUT THAT SENIORITY BRINGS

When the young men on Wall Street bellow across the floor, "Hey babe, great job on the latest sell!", senior vice president Marianne Bye excuses the language as pure foolishness, unworthy of her time or attention. "They're not going to change, so why fight it?" she asks. She has learned to ignore some of the macho posturing that compels certain colleagues to make up stories about their sexual conquests. Marianne even dismissed the behavior of a pathetic colleague who unknowingly bragged to Marianne's boyfriend that he had been intimate with her on their business trip—which was completely false.

When I asked Marianne, "Weren't you enraged by this? Didn't you find his outrageous lie demeaning?" she replied, "I only take action when it becomes an issue of power or control, when the occasional client has the nerve to approach me as a sex object rather than a competent analyst. Like the time," she continues, "when a business contact tried to physically assault me on a company boat in the middle of the day."

Marianne is senior enough to practice what she considers the ideal strategy for sending a powerful message to the man who tried to assault her. She simply told all of her business colleagues about the incident, putting the word out on the street "that the guy is a creep," and she refuses ever to do business with him again. Taking this kind of stand against a harasser exerts economic penalties on both the offender and on his company.

THE GENERIC SOLUTION

Few women are in a senior or secure enough position to take the kind of action that Marianne did. But many have found creative solutions that stop the harassment without having to worry that their careers will suffer.

At one East Coast company, all the senior executives work along a mahogany row, each with a secretary. One morning, ten of the secretaries came in early, at 6 a.m., to cover the mahogany panels with copies of the company's sexual harassment policy. The notices couldn't be missed, and the CEO asked, "What brought this on?" After some discussion it became clear that the configuration of all-male managers and all-female support staff had set up a situation where harassment went unchallenged. The CEO insisted upon mandatory training, which put the offending managers on notice. The women who had been harassed avoided the stigma attached to whistle-blowers and protected themselves from the power and potential wrath of senior-level harassers. No one lost her privacy or put her career at risk.

A generic solution is most valuable when someone who has been harassed and wants the behavior to stop also wants to remain anonymous. This approach is particularly appealing when the offender is a boss, a superior, or a client. It relies on a third party acting as a go-between with a manager in the department where the harassment occurred. At MIT, examples of generic actions include holding a discussion about harassment at a general department meeting, posting copies of MIT's harassment policy in prominent locations, holding training sessions and showing films on what constitutes harassment, or talking informally with managers about how to resolve problems.[5]

Pacific Bell's women's employee organization acts as a neutral party whenever an allegation of sexual harassment is brought to its attention. As Caryn Moir explains, "Instead of hoping that someone will sweep the problem under the carpet, we essentially go in and shine a light on the area." In one case, a woman who worked with the mostly male telephone installation crew found herself at a loss for how to remedy a hostile work environment.

After attempting to resolve the issue through formal channels, the female installer approached the women's committee. The committee, in turn, got the process moving by approaching the company officer responsible for the installer's business unit. Without taking sides in the harassment allegation, they simply asked the officer, "Are you aware that this is going on?" Within weeks, the harassed woman, who had been preparing for a promotion, was upgraded and transferred to a different department. And all of the installers participated in mandatory training on workplace harassment.

Requesting harassment training through an intermediary such as an advocacy committee, a trusted senior executive, or a personnel officer is one alternative to direct confrontation with a harasser. Although a generic solution is not the answer to every case of harassment, it can resolve many without resorting to a formal grievance process. In most organizations, it is virtually impossible to guarantee confidentiality once a formal charge is filed, but a woman can maintain her privacy if she relies on the generic approach.

A woman may fear that she does not have enough evidence to definitively prove her case and may abandon hope for any remedy. "There is quite understandably a strong 1990s concern about the rights of defendants," Mary Rowe points out. "Employers are less comfortable about making career-affecting decisions on the basis of 'he said/ she said' evidence." But, she stresses, getting harassment to stop does not always involve having to prove the case in a formal setting. Mediation, shuttle diplomacy, interruption by a concerned bystander, dealing with the harasser directly, or adopting the generic education approach do not require absolute evidence of guilt.

THE GOOD, THE BAD, AND THE COURAGEOUS: WHAT BYSTANDERS CAN DO

The humiliation of sexual harassment has traditionally been defined in terms of an assertion of power, and sympathetic bystanders can diffuse the power of the offender and the powerlessness of the harassed. The value of a bystander's intervention is that no one need feel adversarial and worry about retaliation. The harasser is, by default, given a chance to clean up his behavior, and the woman can maintain her privacy and avoid career reprisal. Peer pressure matters in every age group: When they witness harassment, bystanders can serve the role of either censor or educator.

Janet Blake* was too embarrassed to tell her husband what a male vice president on her quality work team said at the reception celebrating the completion of their work, "Well, now that we're on the same team, do you think we could start showering together?" Janet's shock and embarrassment might have been mitigated if only the other executive standing next to her had said something like "You know, statements like that offend us all. I think you owe Janet an apology."

In other situations, a statement or question directed toward the offending behavior rather than the offending individual can effectively challenge the rules that perpetuate a hostile work environment: "We don't need that kind of talk here."; "Do you really want to put up that Playboy poster?"; "It's really not a good idea to tell those jokes at the holiday party." Bystanders can perform an invaluable role with very few words. A single statement from a very senior male manager or a board member can be enough to clean things up immediately. It's not always that simple, but it can be.

THE COLLECTIVE SOLUTION

Even when a hostile work situation offends an entire department or perhaps the whole company, women may hesitate to come forward as a group for fear that they will automatically be labeled as troublemakers and find themselves isolated from their male colleagues and from business opportunities in the company.

Helen Wallace* had just joined the management team at a new firm when she was invited to a company party following a local professional conference. The events planned at an off-site conference included a celebration of another woman's birthday. The company birthday "gift" turned out to be a male stripper. After briefly pondering, "What century are we in? Is this really happening?" Helen snapped into her strategic planning mode and called all the women together for a quick caucus in her hotel room.

"Our first inclination," Helen explains, "was to come out with guns blazing and confront the company president then and there, but we decided we wouldn't make a big deal of the incident that night." Each woman decided to go back to her own manager and to explain factually—without emotion—what was wrong with the company picture that night. Helen, as the company's most senior woman, volunteered to speak to the president. When she met with him, she came prepared with a draft letter in which he apologized for allowing the offensive incident to take place and defined the legalities of harassment.

Had there been an enlightened bystander at the party, he might have made a statement—more powerful than the president's—about company standards that very night. A humane man with a good sense of humor could have said to the stripper, "I'm glad you have the skills to dance, but we won't be needing you tonight. I wish you well. Now, could I invite you outside so that you can get paid?"

From a political perspective, a message like this is more likely to be heard and remembered when the messenger is a man. Female bystanders, concerned about using up too much credibility, may be reluctant to speak up when they are focusing on bigger gender battles. And the birthday woman, though deeply offended, does not want to appear ungracious. Ideally, a senior executive, in a quiet and pleasant way, could have quickly dismissed the stripper and proposed a decent alternative: "Let's get some cake and sing 'Happy Birthday'" or "Where can we send out for ice cream?"

THE ORGANIZATION'S IMPERATIVE

The highest cost in reporting harassment is not embarrassment or loss of pride—it is fear of career reprisal. Just the potential loss of good working relationships may make a woman feel that she does not want to come forward when she has been harassed. And when word of harassment allegations leaks out through an organization's informal communication channels, a woman may be ostracized for maligning a member of "the team" or jeopardizing the company's reputation.

How can an organization create a culture that minimizes the possibility of career reprisal and loss of business relationships? What is the best strategy for protecting employee privacy while encouraging the reporting of harassment without penalty?

Training sessions on sexual harassment that say "here's the line—don't cross it" may put a stop to the most egregious versions of harassment. With a strong message from the top, training and role play can also be effective in defining the gray areas for harassment. But it takes more than a stern warning and an explanation of what can land an offender in court to educate people in a way that changes their daily behavior. Diffusing a hostile work environment is rarely accomplished by a single one-time effort.

Provide a menu of options that places discretionary control in the hands of the person who has been harassed—at least for most cases. Recognize that most women who have been harassed are not looking to do battle. They simply want the harassment to stop. The following strategies can set the tone for a workplace in which harassment is clearly defined as unacceptable conduct:

- Do everything possible to guarantee confidentiality and freedom from reprisal for the woman who's been harassed. Once harassment has been reported, watch for any retaliation in the form of unfavorable job references or other negative actions against the person who reported it. Promote educational rather than adversarial solutions.

- Offer generic and problem-solving options: corporate- or department-wide sexual harassment training, office meetings in which a leader regularly reminds everyone about the types of behavior that the organization will not tolerate, regular written communication to all staff members about the possible legal consequences for those who create a hostile work environment.

- Demonstrate genuine commitment from senior management to provide people with the courage to do what they know is right.

Such commitment can serve as a guidepost to the bystander, who can mediate a potentially explosive incident; to the manager, who can require training; and to the woman, who can be assured of her right to be treated with respect after strong action has been taken in response to a harassment incident.

- Give managers and supervisors the support, training, and information they need to prevent or diffuse a hostile work environment. Define their obligation to take action if they observe or hear about harassment: to offer a woman a range of options to stop the harassment, to prevent reprisal, and to get things back to normal after the harassment has been resolved.

- Consider a confidential hot line for information and advice so that women can consult an expert in harassment to determine their best course of action. An ombudsperson's office or a women's committee can also serve this purpose.

- Compose your organization's harassment policy in gender-neutral language. Include remedies for all potential forms of harassment.

What a Woman Can Do

When a woman who has been harassed sees Linda Wilcox, an ombudsperson for the Harvard Medical Area schools, Linda begins by helping her build a decision tree about all possible courses of action, weighing the risks and benefits of each. What is the likely organizational response if you did this? What's the worst that could happen if you followed this course of action? For the woman who tells Linda she feels so humiliated by the experience that "I cannot look myself in the mirror," Linda tells her, "You probably need to do something." Linda's general advice is to choose a plan that stops the harassment with the lowest risk of retribution. As she explains, "The fewer people involved in your problem the better. Ideally, you stop the harassment at the lowest possible level, which is with the offender. If this doesn't work, speak with someone in your organization who you are certain will maintain confidentiality."

With career survival in mind, any woman can conduct her own risk/reward analysis before deciding how to stop the harassment and whether to file a formal complaint. Every woman I interviewed who has experienced sexual harassment advises others: Trust your instincts. If you think you've been harassed, then you probably have. When formulating your response to sexual harassment in the workplace, consider the following advice:

- Do whatever it takes to stop the harassment. Choose an option that feels right for you.

- You may not need to go public to get harassment to stop. You may be able to handle the incident privately and directly with the offending individual. This can take the form of a letter or a conversation. Write a letter to the harasser, even if you never send it. You can use the letter to organize your thoughts for a face-to-face conversation. Role play first with a colleague or friend to work out how you will handle putting the harasser on notice.

- Seek assistance via an intermediary—a boss, a mentor, a trusted senior executive—if you are uncomfortable confronting your harasser directly. You can also send a clear, yet anonymous, "generic" message. Mail the harasser a highlighted version of your company's sexual harassment statement. Post copies of the policy on every bulletin board in your department.

- Put in writing the dates and details of the harassment—if only for your private files at home. Pay particular attention to incidents that can be substantiated by others. Six months after the incident, you may want to read the file to find assurance that you did nothing to bring on the harassment. This strategy may be helpful in putting aside embarrassment or self-blame. And if the harassment should continue, you will have the historical documentation to take action.

- Consider a political approach and a long-term view. When in doubt, consider allowing a harasser to save face. Allowing the offender to save face, once the harassment has stopped, can reduce the likelihood of career fallout. In certain situations, it may, however, be absolutely repugnant to allow a harasser to save face. When harassment involves physical contact or an explicit threat if a sexual favor is not granted, a formal complaint may be the only answer.

- Formulate a back-up plan. For example, "If telling my harasser directly doesn't work, I will speak to my boss next week," or, "If the training that I requested through my personnel officer doesn't work, I will investigate other options."

- Tell a trusted friend or family member what happened. Women who keep harassment incidents to themselves find it can slowly eat away at them.

- Don't blame yourself. This doesn't require you to excuse the injustice you have suffered. If the actions of the harasser destroy your self-confidence, then the wrong person has won.

CHAPTER 7
GETTING RECOGNIZED

"Women who are socialized to ask for what they want seem less subject to discrimination."

—Caryn Moir, product manager, Pacific Bell

Women are, quite deliberately, taught to be humble: Don't show off. Make sure you give credit to the team. It's not "attractive" to have a big ego. These are the lessons through which the behavior of many women is socialized.

Dr. Frances Conley, a neurosurgeon, agrees. "Humility is something women are taught from very early on: Don't get your banner out and start waving it. Yet men are taught exactly the opposite—to advertise themselves."

Merely producing the work required, even when of the highest standards, is not enough for anyone who aspires to a leadership position. "If I just put in more hours, if I just work harder, then they'll notice me" is the attitude many women adopt early in their professional lives. But for women who are poised to become leaders, their reaction changes from "I refuse to market myself" to "Here's a way to get noticed that feels comfortable to me."

Fidelity Investments' Debbie Malins says, "I've noticed that women will work very hard to create something and not take credit for it, while men may not do as perfect a job but will take the credit."

Women, she recommends, "need to stand up and get themselves some recognition." Debbie does not advocate that women walk around and say, "I did this." Rather, she suggests that women first define the direct value that their work holds for others in the company, then strategize about how to communicate the results that demonstrate this contribution.

Feeling comfortable with self-promotion is often a defining moment for a woman in her career. Now that she has reached the top ranks of her profession, chemist Cynthia Friend concludes, "Perceptions of how hard you work and perceptions about your accomplishments are probably, in many ways, as important as what you actually do. I hate to say it, but it's true. If you are quiet and, therefore, invisible, you won't be identified as someone who is competent. You won't be perceived as being particularly successful or having good ideas, which may not be valid, but it comes out that way."

Forty percent of the women I surveyed believe that being a woman has limited their opportunities for committee leadership. And more than half perceive that gender bias has foreclosed opportunities to take on high-visibility assignments. To overcome these structural barriers and to demonstrate their business potential, the women I met have developed alternatives to the traditional male means of self-promotion.

How Men Self-Promote

Frances Conley comments, "I can't tell you how many times I see one of my male colleagues who has gotten a paper published immediately making copies. Suddenly everybody has reprints. I don't even tell my program chair when I have something published, yet for my male colleagues, it's standard operating procedure."

Ambitious women have discovered that many of the traditional male models for self-marketing on the job are simply not a good fit. Male colleagues seem more comfortable tooting their own horns. They'll advertise the extraordinary time and effort involved in completing a project. Women, on the other hand, tend to finish their work, put it aside, and move right on to the next project.

Janet Blake*, an insurance broker, refers to "the complicator strategy" that many of her male colleagues use to get themselves noticed: Announce the project's problems to the whole office, offer status reports, and then publicly rejoice when the issue has been resolved. "They make a project look so convoluted that when they go in and save the day, they look like the white knight."

Janet considers herself an "uncomplicator"—someone who manages away problems and who, from outward appearances, makes her account management look effortless. With some exasperation, she says, "If one more person tells me, 'You've got to find a major problem so you can be a hero,' I'll . . . !" As for such attempts at self-promotion, Janet responds, "I won't do it; it'd be compromising myself. But it is frustrating. My boss thinks my big accounts are easy because the fires get fought before he even has to touch them."

WOMEN AND SELF-PROMOTION

Wall Street's Laurie Hawkes suggests, "Men are much better at self-promoting. They aren't afraid of it. If there's an error made, a woman will immediately take the blame for it and say, 'It was my fault.' But the men will say, 'I did the best I could given the poor direction I was given.'" And, Laurie concludes, "Men are like Teflon in these situations. Women become these mea culpa creatures."

Women are often subject to greater scrutiny when they stumble in a public setting, for two reasons. One is the visibility of often being a minority among the men in the room. The second, as Laurie explains, is not being able to count on someone else stepping in with a humorous remark or a supportive comment to protect them when they stumble; men often can count on each other to be there when they're needed.

In developing a compelling presentation style, Debbie Malins has learned, "You have to be able to step forward with your vision. And you have to be willing to be knocked down once in awhile and come back with another idea. Keep trying until you find a way to make a difference in the organization."

As Debbie says, "Anybody can just talk." The real challenge is to go back out in the field and make your ideas happen. Grandstanding for self-promotion is a far cry from coming up with ideas that will help the business as a whole.

Stepping forward with your own business vision requires a willingness to take risks. Debbie explains, "I try to articulate my vision based on what our long-term strategy should be, how we should be listening to customers and meeting their needs." Admitting that she, herself, is better in one-on-one conversations, Debbie says that speaking up is something she just has to do. "Making recommendations that affect the whole organization can be a scary thing. Some of my recommendations have been very good, and top management has followed them. Others haven't been good. But that's the price in taking risks."

Chemist Cynthia Friend suggests that women can, at first, find themselves intimidated by what appears to be their more knowledgeable male counterparts. "I have heard men make statements very strongly and assertively that are wrong or that they may not be sure about, but they keep upping the ante until someone stops them and says 'That's not right.' They're waiting for someone to challenge them. And if no one challenges them, they just keep going." This is where the old boys' network comes into play; men may feel more protected from embarrassment, more emboldened to take risks because they do not have to prove that they belong.

Cynthia regularly reminds herself: You have to sound like you know what you're talking about. She recommends, "If you have to err, err on the side of being too aggressive as opposed to not aggressive enough." Cynthia also uses her physical demeanor to send a clear signal about her confidence level. She has learned to look people directly in the eyes when she speaks to them and to stand up or lean forward to regain an audience.

FINDING A COMFORTABLE STYLE

Many of us have unwittingly felt our shoulders slump when we see a woman falter in a public situation or visibly show her nerves. On one hand, we may think, perhaps selfishly, "She could have done us all a favor. I wish she had pulled it off. What she does reflects on every other woman in the room." On the other hand, we may conclude, "Who wouldn't be nervous with all these people waiting for her to fail?" or "Nobody does everything perfectly."

Visibility, close scrutiny, and frequent interruptions by male cohorts may explain why some women are faulted for a hesitant style when introducing their remarks to a large group. For example, a woman might introduce a controversial new idea by saying, "This may not be the right time to raise this issue, but . . . ." Knowing that the other men in the room will support him, a male colleague with an equally controversial proposal can comfortably say, "I think this proposal makes good business sense and let me tell you why."

The managerial women I met are no longer worried that asserting their business expertise will be interpreted as bragging, and many have worked on developing a style that conveys both professional expertise and personal confidence. "Leadership is about being able to present both a vision and a style that are compelling," explains Susan Galler, vice president for development at Beth Israel Hospital.

To counteract any potential image of a shrinking violet in the heavily male field of investments, Debbie Malins deliberately adopted a tough, distant business stance early in her career. One day a male colleague told her, "I'm really intimidated by you. You don't seem human." Recognizing that her style had backfired, that she had perhaps gone overboard in demonstrating the seriousness with which she approached her work, Debbie adjusted her style. As she became more confident in her business position, she discovered that "you have to be comfortable with yourself before you can make other people comfortable with you."

Many of the women I surveyed talked about the value in letting their sense of humor show in their presentations, in part to overturn some of the one-dimensional images about women trying to succeed in male-dominated businesses.

Debbie Malins sees nothing wrong with a woman who is aggressive. She herself has become comfortable in taking public risks.

"You have to stand up and be counted in meetings and let your position be known. You can't just sit back and be quiet. I see a lot of women doing that."

Another woman in finance believes that style is a greater factor in success than many people will admit. "A woman's natural working style—which I think is to be more collaborative, less aggressive, less touting your own abilities—doesn't work in some environments. Having more of a 'feminine' working style, as opposed to a more 'masculine' approach, has hurt me in this field."

Women I interviewed candidly admitted that finding the style right for you and effective for your business is not always easy. Like Debbie Malins, others described how imitating someone else's style backfired on them. Engineer Beth Evans* recalls that trying to follow the exact style of a trusted mentor resulted in a disastrous presentation. "I tried a very casual, 'You know, I'm one of the boys' type of approach. It didn't sound professional coming from me, in part because women have to be more careful about professional image. But it also wasn't comfortable for me—so I couldn't reach my audience."

THE GENDER ADVANTAGE

Joanna Engelke, vice president of Bain & Company, a management consulting firm, summarized what I heard from women across a wide range of professions. "I have to work harder than the guys who play tennis together on weekends because I'm not even there when they say, 'I'm looking for somebody to be a speaker at our VP meeting.'"

Joanna's substitute for the relationship-building that takes place over golf and tennis is "to look at the people I'm trying to get to know and try to understand what makes them tick. I can bring some things to the party that most guys can't. People will talk about their personal life with me, while they don't seem to open up with men until they have known them for a long time. So I can take advantage of that."

Joanna has found a comfortable balance between presenting a professional image and seeking opportunities to build personal alliances with potential customers. "In first meetings, there is a level of formality that is important. But I open my pitch with 'I'm so glad to meet you. You probably would like to hear a little bit about me before I launch into the formal presentation.'" If they say "Yes" and if Joanna feels that the time is right, she makes her remarks a bit more personal than just a summary of her résumé.

To make the judgment call about the tone for her introduction, Joanna gets down to the basics. "I look around their office and see if there's something I can comment on—like a picture of their kids—or something we can find common ground on."

Women can also capitalize on the element of skepticism. "When I pick up quickly on things about clients' businesses and come back with some challenging, thoughtful questions that make them think, they're surprised," says Joanna. "And being surprised changes their opinion more quickly than if they expected it."

Accountant Kathleen Ragot has found that her clients seem to perceive her as less threatening than her male peers, in part, she believes, because she uses a more cooperative framework even in the midst of tough negotiations. "I find that clients are willing to work with me and teach me things because they don't see me as being threatening," Kathleen says. "I sense that having a nonadversarial style even helps in terms of negotiating. My style is not to go to a client and just hammer home how many more hours it took us to do something. In the client side of the business, if you show that you're at least open to recognizing their point of view, you can sometimes take the edge off what could otherwise be a difficult negotiation."

OUTSIDE CREDIBILITY FOR AN INSIDE ADVANTAGE

Catherine Lee, a midlevel law partner, has noticed that within any big law firm, "the standard practice is for men to promote themselves incessantly." She describes the norms of behavior that she finds "revolting": "Tom walks into Mike's office and says, 'Mike, let me tell you what I did today,' and then gives him an earful about how great he is." Catherine readily admits her opinion about this ritual. "I hate doing it. And it seems like a waste of time—time that I don't have to spare—to force myself to act like that in order to protect my position. I resent having to sell myself. Whatever happened to 'actions speak louder than words'?"

But Catherine recognizes the business advantage among men who rely on self-promotion as a form of office communication. "The men," she says, "all know what the others are doing since they're always reminding one another of their accomplishments."

At the very point in her career when Catherine began to demonstrate real rainmaking potential, she also began to experience an increasing sense of isolation from her male colleagues. Resistance to women in leadership positions, she observes, is common among men competing for these positions. And the threat posed by an assertive woman may heighten this pressure and insecurity. Catherine has decided not to fight a losing battle within her firm. She explains, "I don't care how good you are. A woman will not be promoted from within. I don't mean promoted from associate to partner. I mean promoted—in terms of recognition—the way men promote their protégés. The only way for a woman to really move up the ladder in any significant way is to build credibility from the outside." And, she emphasizes, "I don't think that's the case for men."

Catherine's professional work outside the firm has included co-chairing the Women's Law Section of the Maine State Bar Association, creating an institute for family-owned businesses at the University of Southern Maine, and spearheading a project on gender bias in the legal system and as well as a program on breast cancer awareness. These efforts have brought telephone calls from new clients as well as an award for her work from the American Bar Association. Once Catherine's name began to appear in the newspaper for her work in organizations outside the firm, "people in the firm suddenly began to notice me; they started treating me differently."

Most experts quoted by the press are men. Women experts, who are less numerous, will be noticed and sought after for their opinions. Getting quoted as an expert, for example, in a story about environmental law or having excerpts from a professional-association speech printed in a business journal brings credibility for you back in your own organization.

Carol Goldberg, former president and chief operating officer of Stop & Shop, enthusiastically advocates judicious use of the press. While there is some risk in letting the public know about you, Carol believes that this form of self-promotion always does more to help careers than hurt them. And she tells her colleagues, "If someone calls you from a newspaper, you more times than not ought to talk to the reporter. Be sure, though, that you know your institution's rules about talking to the press; you may need to go through your public-affairs office."

Talking to the press is a new—and effective—form of self-marketing for many women. Carol recommends, "You do it without sounding as though you're bragging, because actually what you're doing is sharing with others what you're doing and how your work can help them."

THE HIGH-VISIBILITY ASSIGNMENT

Building organizational credibility often leads to the high-profile projects. Line functions are more likely to build organizational currency than are staff positions. Pitney Bowes' division president Anne Pol observes, "If you've always been in a staff job, then operating people typically don't feel that you understand what the heat's like in the kitchen. Establishing a track record in line jobs gets you over the gender issue because you can build a track record that people accept."

Line jobs hold natural opportunities for starting the kinds of projects that demonstrate initiative and leadership potential. When Susan Galler worked at WGBH, Boston's public television station, she decided to take a fresh look at its long-standing volunteer organization and break new ground in how most other overseer groups functioned.

Identifying an unmet need to reach out to the city's diverse constituencies, Susan launched a new volunteer overseers association, which included many of Boston's emerging business leaders. Not only did the newly expanded volunteer organization broaden the diversity of WGBH's development base, it broadened Susan's professional platform as well. This project's high visibility immediately set the stage for Susan's involvement in the station's business strategy sessions. "All of a sudden we had this group of business leaders coming in four times a year to hear insider presentations from the president, the vice president, and executive producers," she says. It was there that Susan learned firsthand about top management's vision for the organization—information that proved very useful to planning in her department.

Now working in development at Beth Israel, Susan keeps close tabs on the volunteer organization she started at WGBH and maintains contact with members of the overseer group, many of whom have become close friends and trusted confidantes. "And believe me," says Susan, "I work hard to stay in touch with them. I call them. I go out to lunch with them. They're my high-visibility network."

Making Yourself Visible

Hard work alone is rarely enough to advance a career. In most performance review systems, there is plenty of room for subjective judgment. Sarah Curran*, a vice president at a large manufacturing firm, believes, "Being astute to the business game means realizing that perceptions about your contribution to your company could be wrong for whatever reasons, and you have to take responsibility for correcting them."

One strategy, recommended to Sarah by a colleague, is to "make sure that you run your own commercials every now and then so that other people notice what you're doing." Sarah admits that she was, at first, uncomfortable with marketing herself. Then she noticed that many women with whom she did business were quietly doing excellent work—often unnoticed by their organizations.

Sarah has discovered several alternatives to blatant self-promotion. One is to be generous in complimenting peers or team members whose work benefited her own. Many of these colleagues return the public recognition when her work helps them. Another technique Sarah has found valuable is using the most effective language to introduce a presentation or written report—for example,

"This represents a major change in the way we deliver our services" or "Here is a project that will have X-dollar impact on the bottom line."

Sarah has also found that when a woman's job quietly expands with little public recognition, linking that growth to company resources can quickly bring her contributions into the limelight. At one off-site meeting with an outside facilitator, Sarah discovered a golden opportunity to convey a strong and objective message about her value to the company when the facilitator opened the meeting with, "Let's put the numbers up on the board. How much of the company's money are each of you playing with?" When it was Sarah's turn, she listed figures millions of dollars higher than the men at her level. "My boss just about fell over," she recalls. "He just never looked at our jobs that way. And it changed his perceptions of me."

Caryn Moir, a product manager at Pacific Bell, believes that getting to know people throughout the company enhances her credibility within her own department. Through her work on task forces and in the employee women's group, Caryn has gained the advantages of both personal and professional networks. "There have been times when I worked for a male boss," she says, "when I have been able to walk into his office and tell him something that is happening before it's official, before it's even a whisper." Caryn herself feels more confident in knowing about big picture issues for the company. And for her boss, Caryn says, "It shows that I have an understanding of the business as a whole."

GETTING WHERE YOU WANT TO GO

The ideal moment to seek reward and recognition is when your performance is at a peak. Wall Street's Marianne Bye is a case in point. "When you're doing well, that's when you hit them for more money. You should never *ever* hesitate about asking for money when you know you are worth it."

At one point, when Wall Street was feeling a shortage of managers in Marianne's field, three other firms made her offers in rapid succession. Adopting a direct approach with her boss, she told him, "I have some offers on the table, and I need to know something. In order to make more money, do I have to leave? Is that what usually happens here?"

Marianne was in an ideal position to discuss a salary review. She had just completed a highly successful project, and she had some real job alternatives in hand. Because she had been on a search committee, Marianne was also aware that a new male recruit was about to be hired at a salary higher than her own. With all these facts to support her, she negotiated an increase that nearly doubled her salary.

Marianne believes, "A lot of times when you try to leave a firm, management responds with, 'Oh, but we made you. We did this for you. You owe us.' Well, that's absolute b.s. If they really wanted you, they would come up with a way to keep you." Marianne cautions against letting loyalty dictate bad career decisions. "I think women are more likely to feel an obligation to stay. But it's got to be your business decision."

Caryn Moir believes that her compensation is, in many ways, dependent not only on her performance but also on how well she works with the decision makers at Pacific Bell. "I make it a point to let them know what I'm working on," she emphasizes. Caryn has also learned to seek out bosses who are skilled at visibility and adept at negotiating organizational resources for their staff.

A year after Caryn joined Pacific Bell, another woman with a nearly identical profile joined the company, also at an entry-level professional position. "Jill* wasn't happy with the raises she was given and the developmental opportunities that came her way," comments Caryn. Jill would walk into her boss's office and accuse him of being discriminatory, of not respecting her, of not communicating with her. "And maybe that was all true," says Caryn, "but that's where we separated."

Caryn advises women to walk into a job expecting to be treated equitably and honestly but to still do some double checking on their own to be certain that they're being paid fairly. But keep a balance when doing this: Focus on asking your boss the right questions rather than launching directly into accusations.

For Jill, accusations escalated an already difficult situation and foreclosed options for moving into another department. To make matters worse, Jill went to her boss's boss with her complaints. As Caryn points out, "She didn't know the rules: Never go to your boss's boss. And this isn't a female thing. Men who do this do themselves in too."

A problem-solving approach could have gotten Jill what she wanted without putting an admittedly less-than-enlightened boss on the defensive. A more effective scenario would have been for Jill to either reframe the issue by bringing her job goals to her boss's attention or, if the situation was truly untenable, to begin networking with women like Caryn to search for a new job.

Caryn readily admits, "Sometimes it takes every ounce of strength I've got not to let people know exactly what I'm thinking or how unfairly they're treating me, but it's worth it in the long run." That being said, it's important to remember that not being an advocate for yourself can hold you back. As Caryn explains, "If I have a fear of speaking up and don't ask for what I need, I won't get it, and then I won't be as productive as I really could be." It's a delicate balance.

Caryn's recommendation? "You need to have confidence in yourself. You need to believe that you are good. And don't be defensive about it. Being defensive takes away from your quality. That's all they see. It's like someone wearing a very nice suit and always tugging at it as if it doesn't fit them right."

POSITIONING THE NEXT CAREER MOVE

Diana Barnes*, a management consultant, has set her sights on becoming the head of information technology for her firm. She has just accepted the position of senior vice president of information systems, working for the CFO in the national office. Diana believes this move will position her career for the top technology job at her firm or at a competitor company.

When I asked Diana how she first heard about her new position, she answered with a hearty laugh, "I didn't. There wasn't such an opening. I created it." Diana knew enough about her industry to recognize the merit in capitalizing on a specialty she loved, accurately predicting its rising value to her company.

In reality, Diana began laying the groundwork for this opportunity the first day she walked into the company four years ago. Having entered the consulting field with a background in technology, Diana let her boss know right away that she thought she could contribute to the firm's information technology goals. Her career lobbying led to special projects and membership on the company's technology committees—responsibilities outside the job description of all the other first-level consultants.

With each trip to national committee meetings, Diana gained visibility in key offices across the country, showcasing her skills in improving the firm's central database and information flow. When Diana first met Mark*, the company CFO, at the firm's headquarters, she found, "We just clicked intellectually." She decided then and there to begin a personal campaign to write herself into a job within the CFO's division. "The opportunities were not immediately there," Diana emphasizes, "so I had to look at how I could create them by making a contribution to the bigger whole."

Before committing herself to lobbying for her next career goal, Diana researched Mark's unwritten credentials as a boss. Ever since her most recent boss began to make comments about the shape of her legs, Diana decided she would never, if she could help it, "work for such a fool again." First, Diana checked Mark's reputation in working with women across the company. "He was squeaky clean." Then she researched his perceived value to the firm. "The people in the field see him as real key player, *and* he sits on the executive committee."

At one point, Diana almost did her job too well. To gain support for a needs assessment of the firm's information technology, she was granted an audience with the firm's executive committee. But Diana had laid so much advance groundwork that the committee approved her written proposal before the meeting was even held. Losing the chance to make a presentation to the firm's executive committee meant that Diana would need to approach Mark directly with her proposal to be the one to implement the technology assessment's results. Although Mark offered his verbal go-ahead to Diana, he was reluctant to approach Diana's boss who was notorious for being volatile about losing staff members.

"Mark had me dangling on the line," says Diana, "so I nudged him with E-mail notices about women in other consulting firms getting promoted into jobs like 'vice chairman of technologies.'" Eight months after his verbal OK, Mark had not yet approached Diana's boss. Having developed a comfortable rapport with Mark, she met with him in person and said, "I'm ready to move and grow. We either make this move now or we're never going to do it." That worked; Diana has the job she wanted. Four years of positioning her career move paid off.

LOBBYING FOR YOUR OWN CAUSE

While it may seem crass to "package" and promote yourself as a product, remember that no one hesitates to market a new program or new product in which she strongly believes. Don't find yourself accepting the attitude: "I did such a good job, but nobody noticed. Too bad." An essential part of your own career self-management is making your business worth known.

Here are some ideas for bringing your talent into the limelight and for gaining recognition within your organization:

- Market your skills by adopting a style that is comfortable for you. Many women feel like imposters when they follow traditions used by many men for self-promotion and recognition. Find a strategy of your own to make yourself visible and memorable.

- Quantify information about your performance for management at every opportunity. Focus on facts and bottom-line outcomes to gain recognition and respect for your contribution to the larger organization. Keep a running log of your successes on the job. Quarterly reports, E-mail project updates, professional publications, and the local press are vehicles for getting the word out on your current contributions and future potential.

- Target points of opportunity for career visibility and skill development. Many women report that they are often tapped for projects like a blood drive or United Way campaign, which, while valuable in their own right, do little to enhance their value to the organization. If you've managed a project like this once, volunteer the next time for a task force or planning committee that's more directly related to the business of the organization, such as one that deals with long-range planning or marketing for a new product.

- Look beyond your job description for opportunities to showcase your skills—on special assignments, strategic committees, start-up operations. Pitney Bowes' division president Anne Pol advises, "Don't wait to be asked. Always let people know when you're interested in making a move."

- To avoid the trap of producing excellent work that goes unnoticed, try not to get so buried in your own work that you're shut out from knowing what others in your department and organization are doing.

- Build credibility with your internal customers, identifying the value your work holds for the people around you.

- Before accepting a new job, research your prospective boss's track record, including visibility and standing in the organization. For instance, does he or she chair any strategic committees? What is his or her involvement in professional associations? Is he or she known for supporting talented people in their professional development? What happens to the careers of his or her staff?

- Share credit and information with peers and bosses. Acknowledging the contributions others make and staying connected within the larger organization can open up opportunities for personal recognition and career visibility. For example, let a boss know that his or her staff supported an important effort in your group. Invite colleagues from outside your department to join you at an evening seminar or professional association meeting.

- Use credibility outside the organization to gain professional recognition from within. Let your organization see the talent you bring to professional associations, women's networks, and community organizations.

CHAPTER 8

EASING THE WORK/FAMILY CRUNCH

"When you are sharing your life events with your place of work, you are really vulnerable as a woman."
—A vice president for marketing and mother of two

At DePaul University, when students were asked to rate a videotaped performance of the same woman, pregnant for half of the students and not pregnant for the other half, "the pregnant employee was consistently rated lower in almost all categories, including maturity, flexibility, and how well she gets along with others."[1]

When Mary Jane Stirgwolt's name came before the Massachusetts Governor's Council for nomination to a register of probate position, she was eight months pregnant. One of the men who would vote on her appointment asked publicly, "What are you? Superman? The most important thing is that little baby and the family. . . . I think you're overextending yourself."[2] The man later apologized, and Mary Jane is now in the job. But his comments reflect a form of bias against women, usually unspoken, that can stall and even derail a career.

Easing the work/family crunch is, unfortunately, still viewed by many as "a woman's issue" rather than a societal concern. Eighty-nine percent of the women I surveyed believe that successful women must make greater personal sacrifices than successful men. Seventy-three percent report that once a woman has a child, she is automatically perceived to be less committed to her career. Ninety percent believe an absence of corporate-sponsored flexibility for family needs contributes to gender bias.

One woman in finance told me that when she moved to a new position and essentially hid the fact that she has young children, her career began to take off. Other women, without children, described their organizations' resistance to using the flexible policies touted in their personnel manuals. Their stories identify the difficulty in legislating policy that requires a profound shift in attitudes.

A part-time trial attorney describes how rigid attitudes affect managerial practice. "Perhaps the most annoying aspect of gender inequity arose at a weekly litigation group meeting at which attendance is expected," she explains. "After one meeting that I and the only other woman in the group didn't attend (we were both in court), the supervising partner sent us memos asking where we had been—something he had never asked of men who missed meetings. I was furious and confronted him about his assumption that we must have had child-care problems. He apologized, but I was left with the impression that I was being held to a different standard. I had to account for myself while the men were assumed to be legitimately busy with something else."

Among the women I surveyed, 24 percent rate their organizations as "very supportive" in meeting the needs of working mothers; and in this group, most work in organizations of fewer than 100 employees. Another 60 percent rate their companies as "somewhat supportive" and 16 percent view their organizations as "not at all supportive" of working mothers.

Many of the women I met said that what makes it possible to achieve work/life balance is support from their immediate boss: for arranging a leave to care for a child or parent, for taking an occasional sick-child day without career repercussions, for trusting that they will more than make up the time for the early departure they occasionally take to attend a school play or a championship game.

LOYALTY AND CORPORATE BETRAYAL

For eighteen years, Ellen James* had given her heart and soul to the automotive industry, doing the job of two people while overseeing 250 assembly-line workers and twenty managers. In return, the company turned a cold shoulder when she returned from a leave of absence that she took to help her mother battle cancer.

Trained as an engineer with an M.B.A. from Harvard, Ellen's credentials are beyond reproach. As the division's only female plant production superintendent, Ellen managed the back-chassis division where the final touches are put on a car's assembly. As a symbol of the confidence that senior management placed in her, they added to her regular responsibilities the job of implementing an extensive reengineering process. At every other plant site, of which Ellen's was the largest, the company hired an additional manager for this internal consulting position, but Ellen had handled so many special projects before that the company decided to again call upon her superior skills in strategic planning and team-building.

Soon after the death of her father, Ellen's mother was diagnosed with cancer. Several times a week, Ellen made the 3-hour round-trip drive to take her mother to the hospital and provide moral support, but her mother's health began to deteriorate rapidly. Ellen describes what her life was like then. "I was doing the jobs of two guys at all the other plants—working 12- or 13-hour days all the time. I had a department to manage. I was trying to accomplish change in a very traditional plant. And through all this, my mother was getting sicker and sicker."

After keeping up this pace for a grueling year and a half, Ellen started to feel the stress and decided to approach her boss with what she thought were two fair alternatives: split up her responsibilities so that she would be doing only one full-time job or work a flexible schedule to ease her commute for hospital visits (leaving early or coming in late a few times a week for a few months). Believing that her first alternative would be reasonable even if her mother were not sick, Ellen could not have anticipated her boss's response. "Go pop a Valium," he told her. That moment clarified for Ellen exactly what she needed to do next: "It was like 'Game over. I'm done.' I decided right then and there that I had to get out."

When Ellen asked the personnel office about the feasibility of taking a year's leave of absence, she was assured of reemployment by a company policy that preceded passage of the Family and Medical Leave Act. And her boss approved the leave as well. Still concerned about potential long-term repercussions on her career, Ellen also approached her boss's boss and asked, "Are you sure this isn't going to put my career offtrack?" He said all the right things, reassuring her, "Oh, no, no. You're thought of very highly. Don't even think twice about taking the time. Don't worry about it." With such reassurances and her excellent track record—an 80 percent reduction in union grievances and a 75 percent productivity improvement—Ellen felt confident about returning to the company after her leave.

But the summer before she was supposed to return to work, Ellen called the personnel office and found that the company had not anticipated her return and the only opening was for a position she held eight years earlier working for a former subordinate. The answers she received to her questions about returning to work boiled down to "Who do you think you are?" Ellen needed to get back to work to support herself after a year off the payroll. She immediately began an internal job search and found a position that involved relocation to another state. But her company docked her, up front, for half the vacation time she would normally be eligible to accrue during her first year back. Their justification was that Ellen had returned to work one week later than originally scheduled. That week, Ellen explains, was taken up by company interviews and relocation details due to their lack of planning for her return.

Once she settled into her new position, Ellen decided to tell the director of human resources about the gap she experienced between the company's progressive written policy and its actual practice. After hearing her story, he admitted, "You know, on the one hand, I am shocked and appalled that somebody of your talent and your loyalty to the company would be treated this way. But, on the other hand, it doesn't surprise me at all. It is typical of the way managers treat people coming back from leaves." He then offered Ellen this advice: "Don't take this personally. This isn't anything we did to *you*. This is just the way we do things."

Ellen's story speaks to all of us who at some point will face the pressing needs of a sick or elderly relative or the even more predictable needs of a newborn. Ellen now regrets that she did not put in writing what she trusted to be a valid verbal contract, backed, she believed, by eighteen years of excellent performance. Embarrassed about what she did *not* do to exert more control over her own situation, she admits that she would do things differently a second time, taking more direct action herself to ensure her reemployment. But, as is true for any employee seeking workplace accommodation, the need for a leave or a flexible schedule often arises when you are at your most vulnerable.

Ellen, from all outward appearances, is still a workplace producer, but she, herself, admits that the motivation—that intangible edge she used to bring to the plant each day—is now missing from her business soul; she is about to leave the industry. Her trust has turned to cynicism. As Ellen suggests, "It would have cost them nothing to treat me with a little bit of humanity." Even an honest, straightforward admission that the company had made a mistake and mishandled the situation would have helped retain her loyalty.

Ellen now tells others who want to use work/life policies that *they* must assume full responsibility for managing them, for putting them into practice, and for making decisions beneficial to both career and family.

PERCEPTIONS ABOUT FLEXIBILITY

Three years ago, Lisa Green* put her job security at risk to set the record straight about her career commitment as a working mother. When she first joined a computer software company, she did everything textbook right in negotiating a reduced work schedule. She applied for the full-time position of purchasing agent, was offered the position, and with fifteen strong years of purchasing experience behind her, proposed, "I know I'm experienced enough to do this job in 30 hours. I'm efficient, and I don't take any downtime on the job. And it will save you money."

For a young start-up company, Lisa was viewed as a bargain, fulfilling a full-time function at a reduced salary. Because her tenure in the company was short and she was one of only a few women hired, Lisa did not react when male colleagues made sarcastic remarks about her nontraditional schedule. "Must be nice to have bankers' hours," they would say as they walked past her office. But, as she explains, "I knew it was to my advantage to work very hard because I was trying, as a single parent, to accommodate my daughter's schedule." After Lisa proved herself on the job, derogatory comments about her hours subsided.

As the company grew and Lisa's daughter entered first grade, she gradually increased her hours to a full-time schedule. At the same time, the company expanded her responsibilities and raised her salary. Lisa's first-year review went beautifully. At the end of her second year, her boss gave her a rave written review in every area of her job but informed Lisa that her numeric rating would be lowered from the highest ranking of "5" to a "4" because she had left work early twice in a two-year period to pick up her sick child at school.

To Lisa the issue seemed so petty, knowing that on these and other days, she had left work with a full briefcase. Demoralized and in a state of disbelief, Lisa reflects, "I was very angry. I didn't challenge the review, but the issue never left my mind. It made me realize that honesty hadn't been rewarded. Clearly this man did not look favorably on my leaving work early to care for my child." From that day forward, the few times a year that Lisa had to attend to her sick daughter or go to a teacher's conference or a school event during the workday, she claimed a dental appointment or an illness herself. But, as she now admits, "I felt like I had compromised my values."

Six months after her review, Lisa decided to tell her boss what had been weighing heavily on her mind. She knew that what she was about to say was risky. She deliberately timed a conversation that would not be too close to the next review cycle, but she says, "I knew I needed to say something." Lisa explains her agenda that day. "I was purposely calm and had my emotions under control, but I wanted to unnerve him a bit and make him understand that he had behaved inappropriately by taking a loyal, honest, hard-working employee and making her feel that the only way to survive was to lie about the few instances that she needed to be available for her child."

In the back of her mind, Lisa thought about the number of times top management had waved a cheerful good-bye to a man leaving early with his gym bag or squash racket in hand. Several times, her own boss announced that he needed to leave early because his wife, who stayed home to care for their children, was ill. With frustration, Lisa observed that "his halo was shiny because he was going home to be with his kids."

When her boss responded that he had not held the sick-child issue against her, Lisa countered, "I have to tell you the truth. Your delivery for my review was 'You could have been at the head of the class, but you had to leave on these two occasions.' I really felt that this was a little bit of discrimination." Lisa will never know the correlation between that clearing-the-air conversation she had with her boss and her recognition as company employee-of-the-month soon after.

Lisa's story exemplifies the negative labeling so readily attached to a working mother, regardless of quality of performance and productivity on the job. And it illustrates a work ethic that values male bonding through sports but denigrates caring for a sick child.

The postscript to Lisa's story is a happy one. After a corporate scandal closed the computer software company, she landed a job in a medical products company. Here, her new boss opened her first performance review with the statement, "I hope you know how much I respect you as a purchasing professional." For Lisa, "the key word was 'respect' because if people respect you, they aren't focusing on your status as 'working parent.'"

THE MATERNAL WALL

As much as women want to keep their personal and their professional lives separate, they can't when they are pregnant.

The simple fact that their pregnancy is visible makes this impossible. Many professional women report hiding their impending motherhood as long as possible, wearing oversize jackets four or even five months into their pregnancies because they're fearful of the career repercussions of becoming a mother.

Emily Powers*, expecting her first child in the same year she will be considered for a law partnership, watched with great concern what happened to the mothers in her previous firm. "The biggest problem for the women was that they felt like they had to prove themselves all over again," says Emily. "When they became mothers, all of a sudden everyone assumed they were no longer committed to their careers and that all they were going to care about were their children. And they had to come back in and work those late nights and those weekends just to prove that they could do it—and were still willing to do it."

Negative labeling for mothers often continues long after a child is born. Christine Baker's* career moved into rapid acceleration once she hid the fact that she was the mother of young children. Sad as it is, Christine admits, "When I moved to another part of the company, I didn't bring up the fact that I had two children and no one asked me if I had kids. I got off to a great start there and was given lots of great business opportunities." After Christine established herself, people began to hear about her other life and typically responded with surprise: "Oh, she *does* have two children. Wow! That's incredible!"

Christine had left her position at another branch of the investment firm when "it became obvious to me and to other people around me that my responsibilities were being cut back." To this day she is not quite sure what went wrong in her previous position, but she attributes most of the career barriers she faced to the existence of the maternal wall, a mother's corollary to the glass ceiling. Christine's responsibilities began to shrink during her first maternity leave. Prior to taking her leave, "I was laying the groundwork for some new pricing and promotion strategies around one of our services," Christine explains. "But the timing is *always* terrible, no matter when you go on maternity leave."

While away on her twelve-week leave, Christine called the office to check on her project and was informed that she would no longer be working on it upon her return. Under the assumption that she would be coming back to the same job and picking up the assignment she had successfully managed for two years, she says, "It was devastating to me because I had a real strong sense of ownership for the project."

Christine, at first, rationalized her disappointment by just working harder and actively seeking new business ventures, but she began to notice that she had to fight for recognition since her return from a leave. By the time she was pregnant with her second child, Christine's self-esteem was at an all-time low. "I felt so uncomfortable telling people about my pregnancy. Then I thought, 'Wait a minute. This is happy news. So why should I feel so horrible about such a wonderful thing?'"

For her second maternity leave, Christine faced a nearly identical set of circumstances as her first, having developed a new business line in which she was deeply invested. To mitigate the career impact of her second pregnancy, Christine told the person who had become her new boss, "I know this timing is terrible, but I just want you to know that I plan to come back to the same job and want to keep my project assignments. Now here's my plan for covering the work while I'm gone." But despite all her planning, Christine came back from a ten-week leave to find that she was essentially in competition with a new peer for her job. That's when she applied for her current vice president slot.

Christine describes how her view of her mother/professional merger has changed for the better as she tells her story about her return from a recent three-day business trip. "My plane arrives at Kennedy Airport at 3:45 p.m. If I hop in a cab right away, I can be sitting at my desk, ready to return three days of accumulated phone messages, from 4:30 to 6," she tells herself. "Or I could take a cab to the other end of town to surprise my 4-year-old with an early day-care pickup and a leisurely dinner and bath routine."

Which should she choose? Going home looks very attractive until she remembers that her career began to thrive again only when she moved to a new corporate branch and decided not to mention her role outside the office as a mother of two.

She is, however, beginning to feel more comfortable in admitting, "Geez—what's wrong with me? I've been away from my family for half the week, putting in 14-hour days, and I'm feeling guilty about not heading into the office!?!" When Christine travels now, she knows exactly which way her cab will head even before her plane lands.

It took Christine a long time to find her own balance between motherhood and ambition. Some working mothers never come to terms with their two often-conflicting roles. A woman's personal ambivalence or guilt about her choices may get tangled up in a constant struggle to prove her business worth and may make her wary about admitting that family is also an important priority. Is it a cop-out to make a conscious decision to hide your status as a mother, or is it merely a survival tactic?

Toxic Attitudes

In a survey of eighty large companies by Rogers and Associates, fewer than 2 percent of workers use job sharing, telecommuting, or part-time options, even though most of these companies have policies allowing these practices. They can't use them because there is too much work and too many penalties, perhaps even job loss, if they do."[3]

The number of people who take advantage of existing work/life company benefits remains exceedingly low in many organizations because most managers have negative attitudes about such benefits, which undermines their success. These attitudes include:

- **The business "success" identity crisis.**
  For many people, being "successful," according to traditional business standards, demands adherence to the "my work is who I am" philosophy. A clear division between the personal and the professional roles no longer exists for most women and for many men.

- **The burden-of-proof issue.**
A working mother is often expected to prove herself twice: first as a woman and then as a mother. Stories like Christine Baker's and Lisa Green's illustrate why so many workers feel compelled to hide the human side of their existence—the occasional sick-child day or attendance at a special school event.

- **The comfort of command-and-control management.**
Unfortunately, the unspoken managerial response to scheduling, and perhaps workplace, flexibility in recognition of family life is often, "No way. I will lose control of my people." Forgetting that loyalty is the flip side of trust, most managers continue to attach the highest possible value to "face time" in the office, adhering to the premise that face time is the premiere measure of professional commitment.

- **A lack of urgency.**
Many senior executives have little reason to promote new rules of work that can support work/life balance while getting the job done. Nothing is in it for them. Unless they have dealt directly with the care of an ill or elderly relative or faced the guilt of sending a mildly sick child to school, most senior executives do not understand how direct the correlation is between reasonable accommodation for family needs and the productivity and morale of their employees.

- **Misdirected corporate motive.**
Even employers who institute what they consider family benefits can exhibit a discouragingly demoralizing lack of understanding about the real work/life issues. The idea that children can be brought to the office on a Saturday or Sunday while their parent is working may be well-intentioned (it does ease the burden on parents to find child care on their own), but it masks the real and still unresolved issues of unnecessary workplace intrusion on weekend family life. And on-site sick-child care ignores the reality that a sick child wants a mom or dad for comfort and will probably get better faster without having to commute for care by a stranger.

- **A sadly absent commitment to social issues.**

  How do managers justify hiring a woman, who is more likely than not to bear a child at some point in her career, when they can probably find a man for the position? In some cases, the answer is because the woman is the more qualified of the two candidates. In others, when the two are equally qualified, gender should not be the determining factor for a hiring decision because anyone—man or woman—can leave a job for a whole host of reasons. And more men in the future may find themselves wanting to take a parental leave or requesting short-term schedule flexibility to find nursing care for an elderly relative.

- **Resentment from senior managers who made a different set of life choices for themselves.**

  The "I had to make these sacrifices. Why shouldn't you?" mentality perpetuates the traditionally rigid rules of work. Most CEOs don't need to worry about responsibilities on the home front since these are usually managed for them by wives who stay home. And some women, who have already broken through middle management and are looking toward the top of their organizations, point to a trend that does not bode well for a heightened understanding from future corporate leadership: Many of the new generation of executives are still men who rely on their wives to manage the home.

THE WORKING MOTHER/MANAGEMENT PARTNERSHIP

Jean Duncan*, an associate director of admissions at a small college, describes the wide range of complaints about working mothers among her colleagues. "There's jealousy. There's resentment. There's martyrdom. But those who complain about the shorter hours mothers work are putting in longer hours themselves, not because working mothers go home earlier, but so that they, themselves, can advance. Yes, these people may take on an extra project that the mother does not, but they are also getting the credit that she is not."

To counteract these complaints about a mother's commitment, Jean consciously thinks about how best to model behavior: first, for senior management whom she hopes will hire and support mothers; and second, for her staff whom she also wants to succeed as employees and as working parents. Jean admits that the working-mother issue can get muddy on both sides of the performance equation: On the one side, there is the mother who encounters unfounded and negative assumptions about her work ethic, and on the other, there is the mother who abuses flexibility and makes it harder for the next working mother to succeed. Jean has lived the first scenario and been a manager for the second.

During one performance evaluation, Jean was given an excellent review except for one negative observation: She had taken too much time off from work to be with her daughter. Jean quickly countered, "But all of those days were vacation days that I had taken with prior approval from you. I was only out once for a half day when my child got sick in the middle of the day. The rest of the time, my mother-in-law or husband managed the sick-child care." After this reminder, Jean's boss agreed to change her review.

Jean understands that perhaps taking vacation days one at a time rather than in a block like the rest of the staff made her absences more visible. Yet she admits that her boss's seemingly minor remark absolutely infuriated her because she had forced herself to put aside working-mother guilt about having someone else care for her sick child—all for the sake of appearance, so that she wouldn't involuntarily be put on the "mommy track."

When a new boss came on board, Jean negotiated a reduced schedule, allowing her to be home two afternoons a week with her two preschoolers. This boss forgets that Jean is not quite full-time, which, she says, "is almost kind of nice because he doesn't expect me to be on a mommy track. And he sends a lot of projects my way." Jean does what she can to ensure that she doesn't get labeled "a second-class careerwoman." During the four- or five-month admissions workload peak, she comes into the office every weekend and many evenings along with the rest of the staff.

Jean appreciates the unusual goodwill that her employer demonstrates toward working mothers and feels frustrated when others on the staff abuse the college's reasonable accommodation for family needs. As a department supervisor, she has had to remind a part-time staff member who is often late, "Look, I do the same thing every morning. We all have to get our kids up, fed, and dropped off where they're supposed to go and get to work on time. You're putting the office in jeopardy when you're not here to cover the phones." Jean is concerned that if this employee breaks her end of the working mother–management partnership, it will be harder for the next woman who wants flexibility.

Despite her own progressively flexible office environment, Jean advises other women, "Don't ever discuss family issues, especially children, at work, unless you're speaking to a good friend." She points to the trap a job-hunting friend fell into by talking about her personal needs before she even landed an interview. When she called to inquire about the job, she asked about the hours, telling her potential boss, "I have young children and my husband works really long days. Can you offer me any flexibility?" When Jean heard that, she told her friend, "You just shot yourself in the foot. You aren't even a candidate yet. They don't want to know about your personal life. They don't care. It makes you look like this wife and mother, which you are, of course. But if you want to be a professional, that's the way you have to be seen." Her friend never did get invited for an interview.

Jean can also point to examples where give and take in the working mother–management partnership has paid off for both. Last year, she hired a new receptionist who asked, in her final interview, about flexibility. "My daughter is entering her senior year of high school, and I know I won't have vacation time when I start, but I'd really like to go to some of her afternoon sports events." Jean immediately responded, "Of course," admitting that as a mother she applauds involvement with school activities. In return, she hired the best candidate for the job, who, for a very short period of time, needed a little flexibility.

Dismantling the Maternal Wall

Why haven't more women been more courageous in blazing new paths for flexibility and nontraditional work schedules?

First, there is fear of career reprisal and worry about job security. Working in a difficult economy, many women are held hostage to a do-or-die work ethic. Far too often, progressive corporate policies lie dormant for fear of what their use will do to a career. Even employees who have quietly and successfully arranged a nontraditional work schedule are often hesitant to advertise its benefits, because they know they are unusually fortunate and they worry about unfair scrutiny.

Second, many of the women I met said that an absence of role models has made it exceedingly difficult to establish real support for workplace flexibility. Having witnessed mothers before them daunted by the huge gap between progressive policies and actual practice, women may be reluctant to deviate from the model of the traditional male career. Even a mother who takes a parental leave and then returns to full-time work finds it difficult to avoid misconceptions about career commitment. She is not given the best clients any more; her name is removed from consideration for committee leadership; and she has to fight hard to keep her career from being derailed.

Part-time work is not the answer for every woman; most cannot afford to be part-time for the long-term. The flexibility that most mothers need is not about reducing work hours, but about changing attitudes. Rather than being forced to lie about the existence of a personal life, it takes much less energy and planning time simply to tell the truth: "For the next four weeks, I'd like to leave at 4:30 to attend my daughter's soccer tournament," or "I'd like to be a den mother to my son's Cub Scouts late Friday afternoon once a month—so how about if I cover the Saturday clients?"

When Judy Walker and I conducted the research for *Women and the Work/Family Dilemma*, we identified "the maternal wall"—an invisible yet powerful, impediment to a woman's ability to successfully merge ambition and nurturing. Even women who had no intention whatsoever of slowing down—women who often were the primary breadwinner in their families—were forced to defend the compatibility of their ambition with their maternal role.

Five years after our study, mothers have noticeably cast aside self-blame in favor of a new confidence in their right—and indeed their ability—to achieve the best of both worlds on their own. The obstacles are still there, but women now know that waiting for the organization to dismantle the maternal wall is ineffective and naive.

Nancy Wilsker, a partner at Brown, Rudnick, Freed and Gesmer in Boston, struggles to maintain a balance between her personal life and the demands of her firm. She candidly admits, "I can have as many kids as I want, as long as that doesn't interfere with 2,000 billable hours." When, in reality, there aren't enough hours in the day to satisfy the demands of all the people in her life, she does the best she can to make sure their real needs are met. Nancy, herself, feels little conflict and few misgivings about her choices as working mother. "I am the daughter and granddaughter of working mothers and know that it does not have to damage the children or destroy your marriage." But she worries about the legacy of fatigue that seems to get passed on from one generation of working mothers to the next. "The stress of trying to 'have it all' is extraordinary, and few women are likely to want to undertake the journey or stay the course. Little has changed to support working mothers. And I wonder if my daughters are destined to fight the same battles."

Other than her three short maternity leaves, Nancy has never deviated from the traditional male partnership track. She finds it demoralizing when senior partners question her commitment. Recently, a senior partner questioned whether partnership and membership on the firm's senior management committee were what she really wanted. "He is completely baffled about why I am doing what I am doing and asked me recently—after fifteen years of working together—whether I would really prefer to work part-time but have been too timid to ask," she says. Sometimes discouraged about how deeply entrenched the perceptions are about limitations on a mother's abilities, Nancy emphasizes, "I have never been too timid to ask for anything, and most people who have known me for fifteen years know that."

Caryn Moir, a product manager at Pacific Bell, uses her feisty sense of humor to deflect unfounded and unwelcome assumptions about where she should be spending her time. After a peer, who she also considered a good friend, told her, "You know, it has always been my personal belief that if you give birth to a child, you should stay home and raise it," her first inclination was to rebound with "And who are you to force your belief system on me?!?" But now, instead of being put on the defensive, Caryn catches men who make such comments off guard with an outspoken comeback. "Would you do that to my child?" she asks them. "Would you sic me on a child 24 hours a day? Think about it. I'm not a good 24-hour-a-day Mom. It's just not who I am."

Value-laden questions about what a mother should be, where she should be spending her time, and how she should be leading her life, even if unspoken, permeate a woman's experience at work. A woman must challenge these assumptions herself to prevent them from undermining career potential.

FLEXIBILITY AND DEFINITIONS OF SUCCESS

In the quest for balanced lives, some women carve out unique arrangements that will make it easier for the next nontraditional worker to succeed. Kathleen Ragot, an accountant at Coopers & Lybrand in San Francisco, explains the unusual life circumstances that led to her current 60 percent part-time arrangement. Her husband, who was in the construction industry, was required to relocate from Philadelphia to San Francisco. "And lo and behold, I discovered that he would need to move every three or four years. Knowing how hard he would be working—and I wouldn't see a great deal of him anyway—I decided to concentrate on my own career and try to stay in the same place. If you change jobs too often, it's frowned upon unless it's the company itself asking you to move." Kathleen put together a part-time arrangement so that she could travel on an extended weekend basis to wherever her husband was, which, for awhile, turned out to be, of all places, Hawaii.

In addition, Kathleen wanted to counteract her own sense that she was becoming more and more "one dimensional," on a partnership treadmill with no real life balance. She had also noticed a disturbing trend in accounting: Many people who put their personal life on permanent hold got a knock on their office door and were told by a managing partner, "Hey, we're not going to make you a partner. So, you should find something else to do."

Before proposing what is seen as a radical arrangement by Big Six accounting-firm standards, Kathleen tested the waters with key partners in the firm. "One of the things I figured out," she explains, "is that although the personnel office might support something like this, if the practitioners don't go along with it, all bets are off." She presented her case for flexibility in terms of how she would meet client demands rather than how it would support her personal goals.

Interestingly enough, many of Kathleen's clients do not even know her work schedule is reduced. "It's relatively transparent to them in the sense that many people travel in this business or they spend a full day in another client's office. Yet some of my clients do know. Their attitude is that they'd rather work with a part-timer than have turnover every few years."

For the past three years, Kathleen has worked a three-day-a-week schedule. Because she does not have child-care issues, Kathleen decides each week how to put in at least 24 chargeable hours. Sometimes she comes into the office every day for a half day of work. Because she does not want her firm to decide that she is too expensive for a part-timer, she regularly works extra hours like the rest of the staff. To be fair to her firm while avoiding exploitation as a part-timer, she considers, "What is a normal amount of overtime hours for a typical manager? Then I should work at least 60 percent of that amount of overtime."

Kathleen readily admits that not having the constraints of day care allowed her to offer flexibility as an additional selling point for her proposed arrangement. She has noticed that mothers working part-time often find themselves in a daily battle with the clock racing out the door—after answering just one more question—and then paying a fortune in overtime day care. Many of these part-timers have left the firm, commenting in exit interviews, "My reduced schedule ended up costing me so much money in extra child care that I had to find something else to do because I couldn't afford it any more."

Being the only part-timer can be a lonely road and, at times, professional ego suffers. As Kathleen comments, "I've discovered that managing a part-time arrangement is perhaps a bit easier in the beginning because you're clear about your vision of how it should work." For her first two years on a reduced schedule, Kathleen contained her hours and never went into the office on Saturdays. In the last year, she has worked many weekends and found herself gradually slipping back into a full-time slot. She knows she may have to set some limits as part of her ongoing evaluation of whether the arrangement is working for both her firm and herself.

Kathleen lives with few regrets about her decision not to suffer burnout by the time she is 45. "I saw my dad retire and then die within the year," she says. "And he was always a workaholic, but you can't spend it if you're in the ground."

BECOMING YOUR OWN ADVOCATE

The one common message I heard from the women I surveyed, many of whom are responsible for both children and elderly parents, is: Don't assume anything when it comes to a company work/life policy. Most organizations remain stuck in bad habits that effectively block the success of such policies. To accelerate the pace of change, here are some suggestions for putting a nontraditional schedule into successful practice:

- Conduct periodic check-ins. Six months into a new arrangement, ask your boss and your personnel office, "Has there been any feedback that this isn't working? Have there been any complaints? How are my coworkers reacting?"

- Don't call unnecessary attention to the limitations on your availability. If, for instance, a client wants to meet at a time when you are not in the office, don't offer an explanation that may put them on the defensive, such as "Oh, I'm sorry; I work part-time and can't make it." Simply say, "That time is not convenient for me. How about next Tuesday instead?"

- Be willing to let go. Some women find themselves so burdened by the guilt of having to leave at a set time that they never fully appreciate the benefits that a part-time schedule is supposed to bring. As Kathleen Ragot suggests, "Some of the barriers to success are internal as well as external."

- Establish reasonable limits. Overtime is often a prickly issue for part-time professionals. Many put in too much rather than too little. But too much overtime defeats the purpose of working part-time. Plan ahead for what is reasonable given the extra hours expected from all employees.

- Will yourself not to apologize for developing a work option that is right for you personally. Alternative schedules, although still viewed with skepticism, hold untapped potential for easing family demands while enhancing employee retention.

- Make it impossible for your organization to turn you down. Put in writing a detailed description of your work plan and answer all the tough questions up front. Give your boss an "out." Suggest a review of the arrangement after six months or, in a particularly skeptical organization, after a three-month period. Propose that if your arrangement is not meeting the demands of the job, you will revert to a traditional schedule at the end of the trial period.

- Confront the political realities of face time. Refuse to let a flexible work arrangement push you off the career radar screen. My former job-share partner Patti Hunt Dirlam, now a Boston-based training consultant, used to remind me on a regular basis, "Get out of the office. Walk the halls, Deb. Let people know you're alive. You can pick up great information out there."

- Document and showcase your performance at every opportunity. It was no accident that within our first six months of job-sharing, Patti and I volunteered to take on the project most highly valued by senior management: revamping every aspect of computer operations and office support.

- Assume the role of corporate educator for putting family-friendly policies into practice. Put in writing and get your boss to sign off on your plan for a leave, work reentry, or a nontraditional schedule.

- Look for and expect no favors. Continue to be the first to see if your arrangement is working for everyone: bosses, clients, coworkers, and your family. Make a deal with your organization that benefits them as well as you—and, if necessary, keep reminding them of these benefits.

CHAPTER 9

WOMEN HELPING WOMEN

"Life as a woman is all about support."

—A domestic-relations attorney

The women I surveyed are using the merits of relationship-building to fuel a two-pronged approach to gender reform. On a personal level, they're helping other women by offering a sounding board for a sticky situation, a reality check on a judgment call, or an experienced ear to sort out the battles worth fighting. On a more global level, they're using the strength of numbers to ignite positive action from organizations to recruit and promote talented women. Women have discovered that by helping other women, they are also helping themselves.

The dragon lady—the harsh image of the woman meaner and tougher in business than men—is beginning to fade from the reality of the corporate landscape. So, too, is the queen bee—the woman who derives her authority, in large part, from being the only female among men. The woman manager who does not help, and may even consciously exclude other women from power, still exists, but she is the exception among the women I met.

As Susan Galler, vice president for development at Boston's Beth Israel Hospital, suggests, "I really believe that women empower each other by example and by mentoring. We have to mentor each other and pass on the lessons that we've learned; and we have to be very open about the battle scars, the successes, and the failures so that we can help each other."

In answer to the question, "Have you ever received advice or support from another woman that made a difference in confronting gender bias?" nearly 40 percent of the women I surveyed responded, "Yes." They described valuable lessons learned from colleagues, professional associations, mentors, and, in some cases, from their sisters and mothers. Many others indicated that with so few women senior to them in their organizations, there have been few opportunities to learn from the experiences of other successful women.

The vast majority of women I heard from described a generous sharing of information and support among themselves. Their responses included comments like "The advice I've received about confronting gender bias provides courage daily," or "gives me moral support" and "encouragement to keep challenging things and to organize other women." The source and tone of advice from colleagues, whose experience at work mirrors their own, can be as important as its content.

A real estate property manager reported that support from other women in her field has heightened her own confidence about her ability to resolve difficult issues on the job. One film promoter said that the most valuable advice she ever received came from a woman who taught her to "see myself as valuable and equal." Others commented that watching senior women handle challenging business situations has opened a new range of strategies that they can transfer to their own daily work experiences—so different from what their male colleagues face.

To counteract invisibility and exclusion from career-making professional opportunities, these women are putting into practice the strength-in-numbers theory. They're taking action to help women at all levels of the workplace and generously sharing with other women strategies for keeping careers moving. This sense of shared purpose, founded on a confident recognition of the value women bring to American business, has come to life in a wide range of hands-on strategies.

A CRITICAL MASS

A 1995 directory of 170 national and 350 local women's organizations reports membership of over 1 million in these groups.[1]

In describing how they felt at a meeting of their women's professional organizations, woman after woman commented to me, "It just feels different," or "I feel like I belong," or "Suddenly, I'm not invisible anymore." Law partner Catherine Lee vividly recalls a meeting sponsored by the Committee on the Status of Women Attornies of the Maine State Bar Association attended by about 200 women and five men. At one point, she says, one of the panelists interjected, "Gee, it's great to be here because I never see women in my day-to-day practice. And to you men out there. . . ." And then, after a long silence, she finished, "This is what it feels like for us every single day." Catherine remembers the visible sigh of relief among women who realized, "No wonder I feel so isolated at my office."

As Carol Goldberg, former president of Stop & Shop, suggests, "The minute people see someone like themselves at the top, it changes their view about advancement opportunities." Business theory has it that once women reach a critical mass in the managerial pipeline, equal access to senior management positions will follow. But the truth is that numbers alone will not reshape deeply entrenched behavior exclusionary to women.

In major corporations, only 5 percent of the senior managers are women, and most earn about two thirds the salary of their male counterparts. Even in the federal government, where women hold a higher percentage of senior management jobs than in business, the pace of progress is abysmally slow.

In 1990, women held 11 percent of these executive positions, up from 2 percent in 1974. A recent study "projects that by the year 2017, even though women will constitute over half of the federal work force and though women receive performance evaluations that are as good as or better than men's, women will still hold fewer than one third of senior executive jobs."[2]

The problem with the critical-mass theory is that its pace, now glacial, will never accelerate without a push from women themselves.

151

While there is great merit in the critical-mass theory as a tool for social change, its weakness lies in a fundamental catch-22: How can women reach the top of their organizations and change the unwritten rules that hold them back when these very rules are what hinder them from reaching the top?

In one sense, the critical mass theory *is* working but not in the way that had been predicted when women first entered male-dominated professions in significant numbers. Women are making inroads into upper management not because their presence causes men to accept them as equals but because there are more women working together to overturn the obstacles they face.

Many women described to me situations in which female colleagues helped them figure out how to handle a customer unaccustomed to working with a woman, offered suggestions on how to announce a pregnancy, or advised them on how to stop sexual harassment by a boss. A manager commented, "Other women allow me to scream or vent my frustration in private when I need to."

One woman in human resources, demoralized about the treatment of women in her company, thought seriously about leaving the organization until her female mentor said two powerful things: 1. "Top management wants you to stay because they respect your judgment—not just because you have good interpersonal skills." And 2. "Don't leave me alone with these guys!"

With a clear caveat about the danger in assuming that all women think alike or that all agree on the need to confront gender bias, women told me that their ability to be heard increases when more women are seated around the conference table. Since most people form alliances and offer support to those with whom they identify, a critical mass in the senior ranks holds the best chance for effecting organizational change.

Carol Goldberg emphasizes the value in women sharing their hard-won business knowledge. "You've got to make connections with other women," she says. "You've got to learn from other women—not just to have a shoulder to cry on but as a starting point for beginning your own research on effective business strategy."

Dissenting Voices

I heard only a few dissenting voices emerge regarding a sense of shared purpose among women at work. One investment banker remarked, "Successful women rarely help other women." Another woman, in telecommunications, stated, "Women aren't very helpful to other women. We're all competing for a few slots." A woman working in electronics described the negative reaction she received from a senior woman "who told me that I intimidated her and that she was uncomfortable working with women." To survive among the many obstacles in almost exclusively male professions, some women have, perhaps, chosen to mimic the men and adopt the exclusionary tactics they use to hold onto their power.

In response to the question, "What advice do you have for other women about strategies for advancing within their organizations?" a small number of the women I surveyed advocated outperforming men. They suggested, "Work twice as hard as the men and forget about having a personal life," or "Don't have kids; work 70 hours a week." An aerospace professional found it sobering when another woman welcomed her to the organization with the suggestion that "I dye my naturally blonde hair, cut it short, get a breast reduction, and wear glasses!"

Collective Action

The strength of traditional male business networks comes out of a trust that's established through personal friendships, after-hours socializing, and a shared acceptance of how business has always been conducted. Until cultural and societal norms evolve in a way that comfortably includes women and men on equal terms, women need to build productive relationships among themselves to accelerate the pace of change.

A united front does not imply that there is a singular business style effective for all women. Neither does it mandate that women draw battle lines between themselves and men. One senior executive woman described the career-isolating danger in assuming an automatic inflammatory stance against all men. "I've noticed in the cafeteria a group of women in management who are very bright, and they've sort of formed this elitist club," she observes. "They meet in a little clique and discuss how stupid all the men are. Men sense their animosity and it's uncomfortable. It doesn't do any good to put down 'idiot men' in such a public way—although I understand it as a natural human reaction by people who have been put down by men throughout their careers."

If not well-orchestrated, collective action can be undermined by being interpreted as male-bashing or whining. The women I met are speaking in a different voice about closing the gender gap, in part because there is no other choice but more important because this new voice is getting results. As their own careers advance, they are putting programs in place that will benefit women at all levels of the workforce.

A POWERFUL VOICE IN THE RIGHT PLACE

Active since the 1970s, Pacific Bell's employee women's group grew out of a concern about the very narrow range of job and advancement opportunities then available to women at Pacific Bell. As board member Caryn Moir was told, "At the time, if you were a female college graduate, you maybe got hired as a secretary. We had women managers only in operator services—that was the 'women's job' in the company."

What began as a group of twenty women coming together to discuss career opportunities mushroomed in less than a year to over 200 members. Their commitment to changing the experience for women at Pacific Bell began with an open invitation for all employees to attend a series of focus groups. Among the questions they asked the groups were: What do women want from an employee organization? How does being a woman affect one's ability to succeed in the company? What does the company need to do to retain women?

From these focus groups, the women's organization learned two things. First, women at all levels of the workforce share many of the same concerns. And second, women at more senior levels may be able to advise women in blue-collar and entry-level jobs.

One of the group's first initiatives was to work with human resources to develop company policy and training on sexist language. A second project focused on improving women's access to nontraditional jobs. One strategy was to offer a range in the size of shin pads and replace the heavy, outdated wooden ladders with aluminum equipment, which is just as sturdy.

The greatest challenge for the 2,000-member group today has been to get the word out among the company's 50,000 employees that an active women's organization exists. Through addressing issues like women's health and offering scholarships for women who want to further their education, the word spreads and the group's agenda broadens as well. As Caryn explains, "It's only through some of our different activities, like our annual breast cancer fund-raiser, that we find out about women with cancer who are having trouble on the job because their bosses are saying, 'You're not really sick'—even though they're undergoing chemotherapy." But, Caryn adds, "Pacific Bell has also recognized breast cancer as a significant issue and has partnered with the employee women's organization to raise awareness and to educate the employee body—as well as sponsoring corporate participation in the Susan G. Komen Race for the Cure."

Talking with supervisors about sensitive issues such as refusing to acknowledge an employee's illness requires the delicate task of giving advice without criticizing. By focusing on educating rather than on taking sides, board members have been able to speak openly with supervisors. When they encounter men who simply don't know how to handle such situations, whose initial reaction is something like "Oh my gosh, we're talking about breast cancer—women's breasts! Whoa! That could be sexual harassment if I mention it," Caryn's group focuses on giving them the training tools they need. Rather than blaming the manager for not handling the situation better, board members like Caryn offer options on how to work with an employee who needs to manage her job as well as a life-threatening illness.

For the sake of credibility and for political survival, the women's organization has been careful not to cross the line into management prerogatives. Instead, members assume the role of information source and adviser when they approach a manager or human resources officer. In the case of harassment charges, Caryn says, "We won't take a side because we're not a witness. We can't offer any credibility to either the victim or the perpetrator. And we need to work with the company. Part of that pact is just to be a very loud voice—not necessarily someone who gives a testimonial." Providing an informal resource and referral service, members will place a call to their ombudsperson or a senior manager to help a woman find her best resource to resolve a harassment complaint. But the group's overriding mission is to serve as a catalyst for change rather than a mediator for individual problems.

Given the current demographics of the female workforce, most of the women on the employee organization's board are middle managers. But this has in no way hindered them from building relationships with company leadership. As Caryn admits, "We don't have the official authority or the power that comes from being in a high slot in the hierarchy." Yet board members have been successful at fostering connections that allow them to pick up the phone with a company officer and say, "Hi, this is Caryn. You know, there's this situation that's brewing in your department. I don't know if you're aware of it, but someone has come to us and described this situation to us. Could you do me a favor and look into it?"

By having good relationships like this with senior management, Caryn explains, "We no longer hear 'You're just whining again.' Nor are we given lip service—the 'Oh yeah, I'll look into it,' and never doing anything. Instead, we have credibility with that officer." And for the woman whose concern they address—be it harassment or resistance to being allowed to use sick time for breast-cancer treatment—she can feel confident that someone has taken her concern seriously. She can resolve the problem and move on with her career.

A GRASSROOTS APPROACH

At First Boston Corporation, the idea for creating a business plan for gender equity originated at a summer associates' luncheon designed to recruit women from the top business schools. Carolynn

Rockafellow, the managing director who heads the task force, noticed that these sessions usually deteriorated into "bitch sessions" about the grueling lifestyle expected from investment bankers. "I just felt these were not very good recruiting sessions because I didn't think they were really convincing anyone that they should work for us, never mind the industry," she says. Carolynn, about to go out on her second maternity leave, volunteered to coordinate a group that would take a hard business look at the barriers that have limited the retention of women in the field.

The task before the group, admits Carolynn, was formidable. "The very existence of a grassroots women's task force started by women leaders as an initiative to change systematic practices, reeducate a male-dominated culture, and promote women's career development is more than unusual in the investment banking industry," she contends. "It is revolutionary."

After interviewing all of the firm's women vice presidents, of whom there were about 150 at the time, Carolynn's group summarized its comments in a written report to the CEO. When the first draft of the report from her committee read like a mere laundry list of problems, Carolynn asserted her strong reservations. "Look, if we present this piece of paper as it is, it will just reaffirm everything that everyone thinks about women whining," she told her colleagues. "Management is not interested, no matter what the subject matter, in listening to problems."

To capture the attention of management, Carolynn's group repackaged its report in a format used for investment banking presentations, asking and answering questions in the client's self-interest: How do issues of gender affect the service we provide our customers? What is the competition doing to attract and retain the best and the brightest women? Can we learn anything from what they are doing? What do the hard numbers tell us about women's importance as producers in the firm?

Recognizing the historically strong tradition of excluding women from the senior ranks of investment banking, the report laid out a series of objectives linked with concrete proposals for senior management that "make good business sense."[3] Asserting that, for a service industry, people are its most vital asset, the report highlighted the lower turnover rate and longer length of service among women at First Boston than at other firms. It also revealed, in clear quantitative terms, that many of the firm's top producers now were women.

By reframing gender equity to focus on the company's long-term business stability, Carolynn felt perfectly comfortable in telling her chairman the truth about women's experiences at the firm after he observed, "Wow! The women here are really doing their jobs." With the numbers on paper to support her, Carolynn responded, "Yes, that is the point we're trying to make. We've done well in spite of the firm, not because of it!"

The First Boston model was successful because:

1. It started out with the premise that any argument for organizational change is more likely to be heard if it's in an economic context. In the case of First Boston, an appeal for social change based solely on the noble concepts of fairness and equality for women might well have gotten lost in the downward financial cycle experienced by much of Wall Street. What tipped the scales of change was the connection made between gender equity and key business objectives.

2. With a carefully conceived business plan, including clear statements on who would be responsible for each stage of the plan, the task force essentially made it impossible for the firm to do nothing. By assuming responsibility themselves for well-defined and measurable goals, senior women at the firm agreed to head subcommittees in the following areas: career development, family issues, mentoring, recruiting, and sexual harassment. To sustain momentum in meeting its goals, each subgroup committed to meeting with the CEO every month.

3. To communicate its message and its endorsement from the top, the task force's agenda was disseminated widely and clearly, through avenues that included an E-mail broadcast from senior management, a company newsletter, and inclusion in the firm's orientation program of new policies on the recruitment and retention of women.

Among the task force's measurable results in its first year of operation were:

- the start-up of an internal data bank of nearly 200 women willing to help with firm recruiting,

- the implementation of a career-development mentoring program,

- sexual harassment training for all employees, and

- a new policy disallowing reduced bonuses based on length of maternity leave rather than business results.

A final component of the task force agenda is to spread the word about the replicability of its program via national publicity, which would be favorable to the firm and useful to other organizations. First Boston's gender equity strategy, the group suggests, "can serve as a working model for any organization and has a universal appeal because it does not require the initiative of management." The only require-ment for a grassroots effort is "a critical mass of women, particularly senior women, who are committed to carrying the initiative forward."

The Women's Task Force, from its onset, looked for quantifiable results to monitor progress and sustain management interest. From 1992 to 1993, aggressive outreach to women from top business schools, recruitment days for top female candidates, and sponsorship of equal opportunity issues resulted in a 33 percent increase in women associates at First Boston.[4]

THE POTENTIAL IN SHARED INFORMATION

Recognizing the reality of the "old boys'" fraternity at work but determined not to simply replace it with an "old girls'" network that would extend the gender gap, many women turn to professional organizations. This is especially true for women in male-oriented workplaces where they are few other female colleagues. Here they find that they have an opportunity to speak openly, without fear of career reprisal, about the frustrations and obstacles to advancement. These networks are thriving in membership. Women leave group meetings with an energized confidence about their ability to do their jobs well and about their responsibility as a trailblazer for other women.

Emily Powers*, a New England attorney, described how she felt the day after she attended a meeting of the Women's Roundtable, an organization founded in 1993 and sponsored by the law firm Brown, Rudnick, Freed and Gesmer. "There must have been 200 senior-level business and professional women there to hear a panel on ethics in government. And while I'm not sure that anything concrete came out of the meeting, being in a room filled with women who are all career-oriented brought a great sense of excitement. As one of the less senior women in my firm, I rarely see so many career-minded women together."

Emily's comments reflect the real purpose for the Women's Roundtable: "To showcase women in positions of achievement and to encourage stronger and more extensive relationships among women in the New England business, professional, and philanthropic communities."[5] The group also includes a service network that sponsors support for community projects related to women's issues. With a membership of over 600, the Women's Roundtable offers panel presentations several times a year on topics ranging from new technology in a global economy to productivity in the workplace.

Not only are the managerial women I met developing the right information to start organizational change, they are also joining forces to systematically share information that will help their own careers. Defining several key points of access to career-enhancing opportunities—leadership training, compensation negotiation, senior-level mentors—organizations like Women in Development are putting to good use the power of shared information. One of its newest ventures is a negotiation hot line through which women can call senior-level women to discuss strategy before accepting a job offer.

Founded in 1980, Women in Development of Greater Boston, a group of about 800 professionals, was formed to advance the careers of women in fundraising. One of the key strategies that emerged through its Equity Committee was to take a hard look at the national surveys that consistently pointed to lower pay scales for women with credentials and responsibilities identical to their male counterparts. The group also paid attention to the disturbing reality that women tend to concentrate in the low-revenue areas such as annual fund work rather than in major gifts and capital campaigns—the areas from which leadership is recruited.

Before deciding on a specific platform for its association, Equity Committee members interviewed executive search firms to try to understand why and how women in fund-raising were missing the elusive leadership qualities necessary for advancement into rainmaking slots. It also asked why women's salaries were so much lower than their male counterparts. The headhunters responded, "Frankly, one of the problems is that the women don't negotiate as well. There is actually much more available to them, but they just don't go after it."

This information ignited a new determination within the group to do all that it can to increase women's salaries and to get more women into senior positions. Women in Development now offers evening training programs to define leadership skills and determine how women can develop these skills, a mentor-matching program in which women who are ready to advance are paired with senior women in development, and formal training in career counseling for the mentor volunteers. The group also offers negotiation training where women role-play about how to get the best possible compensation packages. Its premise is that every job offer—including entry- and mid-level positions—"includes items that can be negotiated."[6]

As Susan Galler emphasizes, "Here we are in fund-raising, and we've never learned how to ask for money for ourselves. Now, we never just refer to 'salary,' because we want people to think bigger. We want them to think about the total compensation package." The group instead recommends thinking about other variables that can be negotiated along with a job offer, including the extent of support staff, the availability of computers for your office and your home, and payment for professional-association dues and for job seminars. The group's manual, *Getting What You Deserve: A Reference Guide to Compensation and Salary Negotiation*, is a resource for women who have to negotiate for their real economic worth. In so doing, the guide conveys one loud-and-clear message: There is no excuse for accepting unequal pay for equal work. With the power of shared information behind us, we need to assume responsibility for showing our organizations how to make this happen.

The Hidden Opportunity Network

Attorney Catherine Lee was advised by other women to "try to create a reputation outside the firm. Then 'the boys' will pay attention." What goes on behind the closed doors of job-search committees and corporate boards plays a powerful role in determining who among the next generation of potential leaders will be sitting around that same table. A small percentage of women have gained a seat at these meetings, and they are making critical contributions to opening the hidden opportunity networks to other women.

Susan Galler has discovered that by sitting next to the right person on a nominating committee, she can adopt an immediate approach to broadening the base of the traditional names that are brought to them. "Somebody will give me a tip about a terrific woman who is on the fast track at a blue-chip organization, and I will float that name to the committee," explains Susan. Without the presence of Susan or someone like her who's well-connected to the Boston professional women's network, that terrific woman's name may never come before the nominating committee and never get a shot at serving as a trustee.

Susan is also a member of the Boston Club, an organization with about 350 members. The club was started by a woman in banking who found that "when all the boys went off to a club, she had no one to eat lunch with." Over the course of time, the group has evolved far beyond business networking lunches. Today, with more than twenty programs a year, it has divided its work among subcommittees to address issues such as the underrepresentation of women on corporate boards. Realizing that it was having difficulty getting women on such boards, it now concentrates on bringing women onto nonprofit boards—often a training ground for becoming a corporate director.

Before a woman is even nominated for a profit or nonprofit board, the Boston Club offers assistance on how to prepare a résumé for board consideration. Tokenism is not the desired outcome. The group's goal is to bring forward qualified women overlooked by informal channels that comfortably funnel men into policymaker positions. Boston Club members are accomplishing this goal by volunteering for search committees in their own organizations, by submitting recommendations to those who chair these committees, and by working with the Boston Chamber of Commerce to identify board openings.

THE ROLE MODEL PLATFORM

Essential to the new gender-equity agenda is a willingness to make time to help other women. While Susan Galler admits that confronting gender bias can exact a personal toll, she finds herself renewed by support from other women who have also been trailblazers. "I wouldn't want young women to think that our generation knows how to do all this," admits Susan. "What I want them to know is that they can turn to other women for support and advice when they hit a barrier. And then they will have the strength to figure out a way that works for them."

Role models are needed at every level and age, beginning with girls to whom future responsibilities will be passed. The Harvard-Smithsonian Center for Astrophysics offers a compelling model for young women interested in astronomy through its publication *Space for Women*. With a focus on teamwork and a message that encourages women to pursue careers in science, the publication features women who are role models in their professions, ranging from astrophysicists to computer specialists to science librarians.

Space for Women recognizes up front the challenges faced by women in male-dominated professions. It also offers hope for their ultimate resolution:

> *Female scientists . . . must often deal with problems that affect their male counterparts far less frequently. . . . Although overt sexism is becoming less common, subtle forms of unequal treatment toward women persist. For example, studies have shown that male students tend to receive more attention in the classroom and are more likely to be encouraged to take math*

*and science classes. In the college years and beyond, the
'old-boy network' tends to promote males and exclude
females."[7]*

The message from female scientists to young women closes with
the question, "What can you do about it?" The answer, they suggest,
begins with a reminder that professional difficulties "may be a result
of the system, not you." You can begin to change the system by
seeking out "mentors, both female and male, who will support and
encourage your work."[8]

This message reflects the attitudes of the women I surveyed who,
in extending a helping hand to other women, first give them a clear
and realistic picture of gender hurdles they may face and then offer
them strategies to overturn these hurdles. Many women report
tremendous relief in hearing that they are not alone and, therefore,
not responsible for the gender barriers they encounter on the job.
No-apologies advice from other women erases the often-lingering
doubt that they might have done something differently to avoid
gender bias or that they should have seen it coming.

A woman in finance described how another woman helped her
figure out how to navigate the male-dominated territory in a
brokerage house. "She was my boss. I learned by observing her
demeanor and conversation. She was always professional, but she
made it clear to men who made vulgar comments about women that
their behavior was unacceptable."

Once any remains of self-blame are gone, real change can begin.

A New Solidarity

Starting in the hallways of their own offices, then at professional-
association meetings with counterparts from other organizations,
the managerial women I met are responding to the need to organize
themselves around a common goal—removing the remaining
obstacles faced by women at work. They begin this seemingly massive
undertaking by determining what their agenda will be and where to

find support for it. Then they focus on fact-finding to support their position and finally to educate others on the merits of what needs to be changed. Throughout the process, women learn from one another specific strategies they can use on a daily basis to break through bias that can hold back careers.

The advice for individual and for collective action is the same:

- Educate yourself first. Then educate your workplace on concrete strategies to remedy the unequal treatment of women. At Pacific Bell, for instance, the women's organization discovered that supervisors who could accommodate men recovering from heart attacks historically did not understand the serious health issues faced by women with breast cancer.

- Formulate a plan around facts that are indisputable. Senior management will always react more favorably to a plan than to a problem. Women at First Boston Corporation went right to their CEO with numbers that showed that women are strong contributors to the firm but that they have higher attrition rates than the men. They also handed him a detailed business plan to support the retention and advancement of women at the firm.

- Focus on the solution, not the problem. Women in Development of Greater Boston identified salary inequity and the underrepresentation on nonprofit boards as two areas where members could take direct action. The group now offers practical information on how to negotiate a compensation package and has joined forces with other professional organizations to bring women's names to the attention of board search committees.

- Establish measurable goals for collective efforts in women's organizations and in professional networks. Assume accountability for meeting these goals. At First Boston Corporation, for example, senior women agreed to follow up with their CEO on a regular basis and to chair committees that address specific issues such as firm recruitment, mentoring, and child care for employees.

- Repeat your message at every opportunity via company newsletters, E-mail, professional-association mailings, and press releases. This accomplishes two things: First, it helps connect women and groups that may be working on similar issues; second, it supports women who find themselves discouraged by gender barriers that persist for them.

- Adopt the role model strategy by reaching out to women in less senior jobs who may not feel that they are in a position to speak out without reprisal. Employee women's organizations can become advocates for other women by educating supervisors and management about their concerns, by recommending training programs, and by advising other women directly.

- Establish links to community groups and to young girls and women who will enter the workforce next. The Harvard-Smithsonian Center for Astrophysics, for example, works with local Girl Scout troops to introduce them to careers in science and provides information on summer internships for girls at the high school level.

- Initiate from the bottom up what is not happening from the top down. Find new points of entry to effect change. This is the key to any grassroots effort. At Pacific Bell, change has come from middle managers in the women's organization who have addressed social issues ranging from education about women's health to strategies for putting a stop to sexual harassment.

GETTING THE RIGHT PEOPLE BEHIND YOU

"I really believe that if women don't have mentors their careers are dead. There are all these little secrets that you don't know until somebody shows you. If you look around, every successful man will tell you about someone—or more than one person—who was his mentor. For women to even get into middle management, and certainly to move beyond, they need to have what men have—a mentor."

—Anne Clark*, a senior vice president in corporate lending

Few successful people go it alone, and women are no exception. Most people in leadership positions had someone, earlier in their career, who recognized their potential, offered an ear for new ideas, and helped them understand the unwritten organizational rules.

Carol Goldberg, former president and chief operating officer of Stop & Shop, recalls her naive response to an early mentor who asked, "Who would you like to have help you on your first project?" Carol quickly responded, "Help me? Don't be ridiculous. I'm going to do it myself." Carol now laughs at her "So you don't think I can do it?" defensiveness, which she attributes to the fact that "I couldn't imagine not having to prove myself."

Now a seasoned manager, Carol tells other women moving through the managerial pipeline, "Rule number one: Don't think you have to do everything by yourself."

Among the women I surveyed, 70 percent have had at least one mentor in their career. Sixty-six percent of their mentors have been men—a statistic explained by the predominance of men in the upper-management ranks. Only 15 percent of their mentors were assigned through a formal program. The rest happened via informal career guidance and sponsorship, usually from a boss.

One manager described what many said about having their boss as mentor. "He included me in all facets of the business. He always put me in front of the client and gave me full credit for the work I performed." An environmental consultant described the "you can do it" attitude from several male mentors who believed in her. "They forced me to take risks, to challenge myself. They taught me by saying, 'watch how I do this.' Then they watched me and gave me honest feedback on how to do even better the next time."

While some organizations have attempted to formalize mentoring programs, these relationships probably work best at entry and lower professional levels where the required knowledge base is clearer and more specific. One lawyer selected for a formal mentor program commented, "There was no natural chemistry or real synergy and my assigned mentor didn't put much effort into it. Therefore, it was not helpful." But another woman, assigned to a senior woman in a real estate firm, had a very different experience and says, "She was an excellent role model for a woman executive."

Ninety percent of the women I surveyed believe that an absence of female role models perpetuates gender inequity. Many are now themselves becoming role models and mentors for less senior women. On Wall Street's highly male turf, Marianne Bye believes a woman's career survival depends upon alliances with her female colleagues. "If you don't get along with the other women, you're doomed," she says. "If you're identified as a woman who isn't a friend to other women, you'll have no friends at work. Eventually someone will go after you here and having a support structure in the other women can be helpful. The men don't seem to support each other in the same way."

Chemist Cynthia Friend points to the danger in never being exposed to female role models and mentors. "If you are isolated, that's when you can start blaming yourself for the effects of gender bias," she observes. Although Cynthia never had a female mentor "because there were no women around," she believes strongly in the role model strategy. "Just by watching me, my female students see how I handle adversity. I'm not bothered by little things. They see me be aggressive when it's necessary, even though I try to foster cooperation most of the time. So they learn indirectly how women can lead."

Negative connotations attached to the concept of mentoring linger, no doubt, because of the fact that women in many professions still need to prove to men that they belong. Mentoring, for some women, may suggest that they need special help or protection because of a deficiency in talent or skills. But the value of mentoring to many women—ensuring access to the same opportunities open to their male counterparts—is quite different. They view career guidance as a strength, not a weakness.

In the days when most people would stay with one or two organizations for an entire career, mentoring often typified long-term business friendships. And more often than not, it was the mentor who singled out a brilliant young protégé and took pride in steering his career in the right direction. In a radical departure from this scenario, women today actively seek their own mentors to introduce them to challenging opportunities, to provide reality checks on office politics, and to gain support for the next project or career move.

Mary Rowe, ombudsperson at MIT, suggests that women and men need not even like their mentors. To consider the broadest possible pool of mentors, she says, forget about finding a saint or a role model you will want to emulate in every respect. Her advice is utilitarian. "Anyone can help you as long as the person is competent and responsible." And she recommends, "Seek out several mentors. . . . Nobody is, or can be, perfect at everything. You may learn different things from different people."[1]

THE GENDER GAP IN THE MENTORING CONNECTION

Among the women I surveyed, 57 percent believe that their gender has limited their opportunity to have a mentor. Some men may hesitate to invest career support in someone who they worry will take time off to have children. Others fear perceptions of impropriety for devoting individual attention to a young woman.

One female engineer points to the challenge in finding mentors in heavily male-oriented fields. "Mentoring presents difficulties for the sole woman at the top. In some ways it can devalue the women she's trying to mentor because others assume that she's supporting these women just because they're women. Sometimes it's better if we can find a helpful man as our mentor instead. It makes a much bigger impact because people figure we must have already proven our credibility to him."

The higher women rise, the more difficult it is to find a mentor— male or female. Engineering manager Carol Reukauf found it easier to find a mentor earlier in her career when her status was more junior. Now that she has reached upper-middle management, "many potential mentors are competitors" and all her prospects are male.

The natural tendency to gravitate toward people most like us limits, for many women, the kind of mentoring that easily evolves among men in the office. The roots of a personal connection, often the foundation for career support, take hold in places less comfortable for male/female business interaction. For men, mentoring often begins on the golf course, through socializing on a business trip, or over a drink after work. This is where mentors open the doors—literally and figuratively—to prospective clients. When a man invites his younger male colleague to an informal gathering with a client—over a glass of beer or at a sports event—it comes as no surprise that this young colleague is later asked to join a more formal client session or to make a presentation at the next important meeting. For women, one of the greatest challenges is to find viable alternatives to such door-opening opportunities. Another is to avoid pitfalls unique to women mentored by men, yet often out of their control: the perception of impropriety and the danger of paternalism.

Marianne Bye takes a cynical view of some of the support she received early in her career from men whose approach was paternalistic rather than professional. "I can think of instances where they thought of me as the cute young girl who was good for chitchat, but their tone dramatically changed back to business the minute a guy joined us." In hindsight, Marianne says, she should have aggressively moved these conversations away from discussions about the weather to pointed questions about profit margins. "These were usually incidents that occurred with corporate management of companies I was investigating rather than the Wall Street types. Women are better accepted on the Street as serious professionals than they are in most corporations."

Marianne recalls, in particular, the elderly board chairman who would take her by the hand whenever they moved from one room to the next. He also took her to lunches where she would be among the first to hear about new business ventures. "I was really uncomfortable when he took my hand and I used to pull it away, but he clearly wasn't thinking of me as a plaything—more as a young girl. It would have been awkward to make an issue of it, so I put up with it because of the information I got and because he was truly an interesting person and a friend in many respects." But Marianne sees more harm than good in this father-daughter model. Although in some respects it was useful to her career, the relationship made her professionally uncomfortable because she occasionally felt more like an opportunist rather than an inspired rising star.

For other women, stereotypes about men and women at work can derail an otherwise productive and professional alliance. At 36, Anne Clark oversees the most profitable division of a large commercial banking network. Even as a single woman, deeply serious and committed to professional advancement, her behind-the-scenes career history reveals how gender can become a roadblock to the kind of mentoring so readily available to men.

In Anne's case, her boss and mentor began to introduce her to key people in the industry—lawyers and business-referral sources— just as she was making the transition into middle management. Her boss's support offered Anne a prime opportunity to develop her own solid client network. "He gave me tons of responsibility—projects where he would just say, 'Go run with this.' He took me to bigwig gatherings and made sure I was included in meetings and introduced as a real player." Anne, in return, outproduced all of her colleagues at the bank, helping her boss look good as well.

Neither Anne nor her boss anticipated the stern warning they received from the head of human resources, who told them that her mentor's career help gave the appearance that he was playing favorites. More troubling to Anne was the implication of an illicit affair between the two; such a relationship never even crossed Anne's mind nor that of her older mentor, whom she describes as "someone like my father."

Her boss broke the bad news to her. "Anne, I'm really sorry, but I'm going to have to back off from helping you," he told her. "There are these ridiculous rumors floating around about you and me." Stunned by this news from someone whose wife and family she had come to know, Anne found herself furious that men her age could spend as much time as they wanted with her boss and no one would even notice, while all sorts of innuendoes and accusations were being made about her relationship with him. And from a business perspective, she hated the idea of losing out on many of the golden client opportunities that take place outside of the office.

From that day forward, Anne found that her relationship with her boss changed in subtle ways not apparent in the short run. Her boss was less likely to invite her to the dinner with business leaders, to be the confidential sounding board for the high-risk venture, or to point out the pressure points with prospective clients. Although Anne's career remained on a fast track, she lost—for no good reason—some of the long-term benefits that stem from a close and productive business partnership.

To this day, Anne remains friends with her mentor, who has since retired. She calmly reflects, "I was cut loose at the age of 32, and I'm still doing fine. I'm glad I at least had some time to learn from a mentor skills that I can take with me no matter what." And Anne herself makes a concerted effort to help other women moving through the management pipeline.

So Long, Queen Bee

One young lawyer, disappointed by the absence of senior women she would like to emulate, told me, "The women partners in my firm aren't married and don't have kids. They seem to have the attitude: 'Well, I made it, so you can too. Nobody helped me, so I'm not going to help you.' They're not the kind of women I ever want to be like."

Fortunately, not all corner-office women are like that. Susan Galler, vice president for development at Beth Israel Hospital, is different. Susan belongs to two Boston women's groups—Women in Development of Greater Boston and the Boston Club— that have joined forces to move women into business leadership and board membership. Being well-connected has resulted in women moving into key positions in Boston organizations, including spots on several boards. "When a woman wants a job, we all pull together and help her get it," says Susan. "We introduce her to the people she needs to know and get her background information on the job. We also have contacts outside our own organizations that can help other women."

The Boston Club, a 350-member businesswomen's organization, sponsors CEO breakfasts where members hear firsthand from business leaders. One subgroup, the Enterprise Council, offers expert assistance on business plans and start-up ventures. Lawyers, accountants, and others will critique a woman's business plan and offer technical support. Another, 50 Something, focuses on issues unique to women in their fifties and sixties. (You can read more about both of these groups in Chapter 9.)

BREAKING THROUGH THE INNER CIRCLE

Getting the right people behind you requires getting the right people to believe in your value to the organization. And to do this, you first have to break through the "we trust who we know" attitude that fortifies traditional inner business circles so often still closed to women. As linguist Deborah Tannen suggests, "Influence flows along lines of affiliation and contact,"[2] and "connections equal advantage."[3]

The women I met are finding alternatives to the ways men enter the inner circles in their organizations. Susan Galler admits, "If I wanted to be the schmooziest of all fundraisers, should I learn to play golf? Sure, but it's not me. I'm not going to turn myself into somebody else." Before Susan enrolled in a negotiation training program to enhance her persuasive skills, she thought she would have to change her management style to deal with several primarily male groups. But after completing the course, she arrived at a different conclusion. "You know what I learned?" she said. "I have to be myself, but I have to be more creative about how I get my ideas on the table. And I have to be willing to take some conversational risks."

By positioning every statement they make in a meeting or public setting within the context of organizational goals, women managers are establishing the credibility they need to forge productive business connections. Susan observes, "Really successful women know how to frame what they say in terms beneficial to the organization." Rather than beginning statements with "In my department, we're doing this," they frame their ideas in the context of their service to the institution: "It's a good idea to take a look at this because it will help the organization in the following areas, and this is the role my department can play in getting us there."

To counteract the command-and-control leadership style common to the senior men with whom she works, one woman manager invokes the cloak of authority from others who back her position. "When one of these guys tries to shove something down my throat, I sometimes have to say, 'I know you have a different point of view, but as we've discussed before, I've shared your view with the president and chairman and they see it differently, just as I do.'" Putting her own ego aside—and instead using someone else's position of authority to support her own—depersonalizes the disagreement and gives her the result she wants. As this manager concludes, "I can never change these people who are so set in their ways and have trouble accepting women in management. So I have to be skillful at finding other ways to be credible. It doesn't demean me. It just shows that I'm smart."

Management consultant Diana Barnes* uses support from above and below to build connections at all levels of her firm. About to accept her third promotion, she continues to focus on extra assignments that get noticed throughout the company. "I need exposure in this company to go anywhere. If I just sit in my office and do a good job, I will get a thimbleful of recognition. But if I want to go anywhere in the company, I've got to do more. I need exposure at all levels—from the receptionist who refers phone calls, all the way up to the CEO who looks for rising stars."

Diana has also concentrated on building a reputation founded on offering help to those who have supported her. "I don't want to be known as the aggressive bitch who plowed her way to the top and ignored everybody else along the way," she says. "I don't think that approach gets you very far in the long run."

PEER MENTORING

With flattened management pyramids, cutbacks in consulting resources, and a surge in lateral job moves, trading expertise with peers makes good business sense. Many women I talked with rely on their informal support network to float a new idea, to enlist technical assistance, or to gather information on the feasibility of a new business strategy. Role-playing with a trusted colleague can reframe a problem with a boss into a conversation that never actually takes place. One woman referred to the sigh of relief she felt after venting with a trusted colleague. "At least I know it's not me. It's the organization that's crazy!"

Susan Galler picks up some of her best business strategies through watching the woman sitting next to her. Sometimes peer advice can be as simple as sharing strategies on how to respond to a difficult situation. For example, when someone screams at her on the telephone, Susan uses the line a colleague gave her: "The only person I allow to talk to me like that is my mother."

College administrator Mary McAteer Kennedy feels strongly about the value of peer mentoring. "When something isn't working quite right for one of your peers," she says, "you may be the one with the expertise to back them up." In her own case, a senior manager referred another woman to Mary, telling her, "I know Mary had the same problem in her department. Why don't you talk to her about how she handled it?"

After Mary shared her own recent experience that involved a thorny personnel issue, the other manager said, "Great! Now I know I'm headed in the right direction." And these strategy sessions have become reciprocal. When Mary needed to figure out how to provide 200 more hours of monthly coverage with absolutely no increase in staff, she asked her colleague to essentially serve as an internal consultant. "I wanted my staff to be able to talk openly and honestly—without any of their managers around—about how the work increase was going to affect them ." While her colleague, in the role of a neutral facilitator, met with the department's support staff, Mary met with all the managers. By the end of the day, Mary had gained honest feedback from two groups with many similarities and some different, but valid, perspectives. With her colleague's help, she was able to call the two employee groups together to say, "This is what you're saying. This is what the other group said. Now how do we take these two sets of ideas and work them into one plan?"

Gaining Your Boss's Support

For Carole St. Mark, now CEO at Pitney Bowes and an early trailblazer in the executive suite, her mentors were bosses who were willing to take a chance on her by offering her key business assignments. "They had the guts to put me in a job that no woman had ever held before and then they defended that decision."

Joanna Engelke, a vice president at Bain & Company, believes in the symbiotic convenience of making your boss's life easier by figuring out what he or she needs most from your support. "It's a rule of thumb," she says, "that a boss needs subordinates who are loyal and who will go the extra mile. And subordinates, in turn, need a boss who's loyal and who will back them up. You can't have one without the other."

Joanna recalls how, as an inexperienced consultant, it was absolutely critical to work for a boss who genuinely wanted her to succeed. In a business where presentation skills can determine who gets the client, Joanna received some tough but invaluable advice from her boss. "One thing I want to tell you is that you should never ever for the rest of your life in a business meeting use the words 'quantitative analysis' or 'methodology' again," her boss advised. "Find a different way to talk about finance. You sound like some kind of analytic nerd rather than a seasoned business person."

Now a natural at client presentations, Joanna recognizes that gaining the skills she learned in business school was a small piece of the success puzzle. Her boss helped her to package these skills to fit their business.

Carol Reukauf, an aerospace project manager, realized that she needed to lay some careful groundwork to gain her boss's support. In her exclusively male environment, Carol's isolation from the organization's social networks presented a serious liability to her career advancement. Her boss, however, seemed a realistic ally open to supporting her career, albeit one unaccustomed to working with women in professional roles.

About six months into a temporary assignment as her boss's deputy, Carol recognized that her boss clearly valued her technical skills, but he "didn't know whether he could trust me." She wanted her boss to feel comfortable enough with her to be able to walk into her office, the way he does with the men at Carol's level, and say, "Phew. It's been a terrible day. Here's what went wrong."

When Carol decided that she wanted her interim job to become permanent, she concentrated on alternative points of access to gain her boss's trust. She knew that the traditional male points of contact with her boss would never be part of her career experience. "If I were his golfing partner, he would have gotten to know me gradually. If I were his car-pool buddy, he would have slowly gotten to know me. But I'm never going to be his 'buddy,'" she observes. "I think managers pick people whose faults they already know so they are aware up front how to work around these faults. Not knowing someone well enough to know their weaknesses carries a higher risk."

Carol wanted her boss to figure out for himself whether or not she was valuable to him and to the organization. To minimize his perceived risk in appointing the first woman ever to a critical and visible position, Carol set out to educate him. "I had to think through the confidence I conveyed, my demeanor, where I sat, the kind of information I brought to him about the staff, what I revealed to him about me personally." Carol also tackled "the tough jobs and did them well," saving her boss, in one case, from dealing with a difficult manager, and, in another, saving him time by taking over a cumbersome reengineering project.

Her strategy worked. Her boss evolved into a mentor.

AVOIDING POLITICAL LAND MINES

Every organization has certain eccentricities, certain rituals that dictate how decisions are made and how alliances are formed. Few can survive office politics and organizational expectations without trusted business alliances. Jane Griffin*, an insurance sales manager from California, described to me how two male mentors helped her separate the myths from the truths about corporate life. "They taught me how to play corporate chess. In essence, they would say, 'Things are not as they appear to be. Let me tell you what's really going on here. Here are the politics behind the decision-making process.'"

Without fear of looking weak or incompetent, Jane could ask her mentors, "I don't understand this at all. Can you teach me what I need to know?" Jane was also fully comfortable with the brutally honest criticism from one mentor who didn't hesitate to tell her, "You know what, Jane? You're really screwing up in the following areas." Jane feels grateful for the toughness and directness of feedback that most women in business do not have.

Diana Barnes says her most valuable alliances have been with a female former boss and two senior women. They have given her advice about the company's unwritten rules, about territorial battles, and about who is aligned with whom. An unspoken rule they shared with her, for example, is not to question the CEO in a meeting. "He acts like he wants open debate, but he doesn't." And they've given invaluable advice on how the organizational chart really works: "These are the key players. Here's how they communicate. And let me tell you about their hot buttons." Although Diana says her trusted advisers have never told her precisely how she should behave, they provide information on company politics with the attitude: Take it and run with it.

Anne Pol, a division president at Pitney Bowes, describes how easy it is to wander into hostile territory and to unknowingly hit an organizational sore point. Anne's mentors have alerted her to explosive situations that could have undermined her success: "Certain things always backfire with that person or that part of the organization, and here's why," or "This is the political mess that has to be addressed. These are the land mines you don't want to step on."

Anne recalls one instance where she had to fire someone whose family was very influential in the community. Because of the person's connections, Anne informed several people above her before she took any action. One of them gave Anne the political information she needed to be prepared for fallout from her actions. Having that information helped Anne prepare for a political storm she knew would pass—with the backing of those above her.

Viewing herself as teacher and coach as well as manager, Anne is diligent about passing on political information that will help her staff succeed. Her goal is to help them avoid havoc, if at all possible, and warns them, "Make sure you handle this extra carefully. Be sure you cover all your bases and talk to all the right people on this project." For the most sensitive issues, she makes sure that her chairman and other top managers are informed and that she has their support before proceeding.

BLOCKING SABOTAGE

Beth Evans*, an engineer in an international firm, found the value in getting to know senior women outside her own department early in her career. There are certain situations when everyone needs a protector senior in the organization. After Paul*, a very young, very ambitious account executive tried to make her look bad in front of clients, Beth decided to confront him in private, because, she explains, "You can't say anything in front of a client because it makes all of us look bad."

Beth waited for Paul to return to his office, where she told him, "Don't you ever do that again. You made it look as if I was responsible for something both of us know full well I had nothing to do with. The client knows as well, so you're not pulling the wool over anyone's eyes." The next week, Paul asked Beth if she would join him to meet with a new prospect. When Beth asked, "Would you like me to prepare a formal presentation?" Paul said, "Oh no. We don't want you to talk. We just want you available should any technical questions come up."

The day of the meeting, Beth was surprised to see three senior people from her company in the room. She was flabbergasted when Paul opened the session by remarking, "I'm here to tell you about our proposal for handling your program. But before I do that, I want to introduce Beth, who will talk about our management goals." As Beth recalls, "Here are three company directors in the room and I have nothing prepared!" Deciding that winging a response would make her look utterly incompetent, Beth began her remarks by saying, "I was told that I would be here merely to answer questions, but let me tell you the process we will use to custom design a program for you."

When Beth confronted Paul for this second attempt to undermine her credibility, his glib response was, "Isn't the important thing about being a consultant being able to improvise?" Paul then began a bad-mouthing campaign about Beth so aggressive that her boss asked her about it. Beth's boss then suggested that she see a senior woman who had been an informal mentor and who had a direct line to the company president. When her mentor heard about Paul's sabotage, she told Beth, "Come and work in my office today. You need to keep a low profile while I take care of this." With her mentor's intervention, Paul's attacks stopped immediately.

When Paul later approached Beth about a new account, he said, "I know we've had some misunderstandings in the past . . ." but Beth interrupted with, "I'm not sure we have had misunderstandings, but I want to make sure nothing like this ever happens again. From now on, if you need anything from me, put it in writing."

Today Beth is a regional manager and has another story to tell about career sabotage—one in which she was the person to stop it. Recently, she encouraged one of her male managers to hire a young female engineer, with a directive that he support and encourage the careers of everyone on his staff, including the newest recruit. As chance would have it, one of Beth's friends happened to be in the men's room at a professional conference, where this particular manager began boasting about how long it would take to "scare off the woman." Her friend immediately called Beth to warn her about the manager's hostility.

When it came time for performance reviews, Beth told the manager that he would receive no raise because he was not a good supervisor. Among the deficiencies she noted was his failure to support the new female engineer. When he tried to deny this, Beth repeated verbatim the comments made in the men's room. "To this day, he has no idea how I heard about his men's room conversation, but he has suddenly taken a new interest in supporting the women on his staff."

OPENING THE FEEDBACK AND INFORMATION LOOP

Without a trusting relationship with you, there is no way that people will come forward to share advice and strategy that can help you succeed in your organization. To foster such trust and bring herself into her organization's informal communication networks, Sarah Curran*, a vice president at a large manufacturing firm, opens information loops by generously sharing with others whatever she has to offer from her technical field and her circle of professional contacts. She advises other women, "You have to become a source of insider information. One of my strategies is to share knowledge with people rather than hoard it. If I get 2 feet of mail a day, I run through it and route things to other people throughout the building—information on the industry, business tips, seminar invitations, magazine articles."

In a highly competitive environment, Sarah has observed that many colleagues seem reticent to share business knowledge, but she has also noticed that most people who receive information appreciate it. "And some day, they're going to remember it—to include me in a meeting, to treat me with respect when the next person doesn't, or to back me up when I need it. Being a source of information is an important key to being included in other private business circles."

I asked Carol Goldberg, a former company president and chief operating officer, how she gained access to the traditional "male" experiences that propel careers forward: the hot assignment that will make you shine, the opportunities for self-marketing, the chance to build business alliances. Carol's response? "I had a terrific mentor inside the company—a bright, shrewd, tough guy who understood that for anybody to succeed, they need feedback. And boy, I got it in spades. Baseball bats actually!" And she emphasizes, "As tough as it was, it was the advice I appreciated most."

Carol also believes that male managers have no reason to hesitate in telling women the truth, be it good or bad. "I don't believe in the myth that women don't have a thick enough skin for criticism. The ambitious ones want feedback. The ones who want to succeed find a way to get feedback."

For Carol, the tough-talking advice she heard thirty years ago, when she made a misstep or two early in her career, rings true and clear today. She recalls how she mishandled a tense moment in a meeting back then. The conversation became so offensive to her that she stood up, banged her fist on the table, and shouted, "No way will I do what you're suggesting!" Then she marched out of the room.

An hour after her unexpected exit, Carol's mentor called to schedule an all-afternoon meeting. This was the session where her mentor, Carol says, "tore me apart finger by finger, toe by toe, limb by limb" for offending every single person at the meeting. At the end of that exhausting session, Carol's mentor said, "Well, we've reviewed for four hours why what you did was not a good idea. But between you and me, what you did was fabulous; that man deserved it and no one else had the guts to do it."

There are rules for fighting back in any culture. Carol had survived this particular skirmish, but her method was not something she could use more than once. The next time she needed to take a stand, she did it behind closed doors in a one-on-one with the person who created problems for her.

Not every woman can find a mentor when she really needs one, and the new career option of "renting-a-mentor" reflects this reality.

Women looking toward the top of their organizations can now pay consultants to walk them through a client presentation, to polish skills in public speaking, or to prepare for performance reviews.[4] Susan Galler has never been afraid to invest in herself. Every once in awhile, she pays for private coaching to fine-tune her strategy on key career issues: how to break through middle management to a vice presidency, how to present a plan for restructuring her department, how to arrange each of her maternity leaves.

THE ALLIANCE STRATEGY

The ability to forge alliances determines, more than anything else, who gains access to the next important career opportunity. As alternatives to the traditional mentoring networks open to men, women in organizations ranging from consulting firms to nonprofit organizations are taking assertive steps to build trusting and productive relationships. They are finding supporters in bosses, peers, and senior women who can alert them to political land mines in their organizations and act as confidential sounding boards for their careers. And they are building coalitions to identify and promote other talented women. Here are some of the ways they've been able to get the right people behind them—ways that you can, too:

- Promote your accomplishments on the job within the context of how your work meets the broader vision of the organization.

- Make your boss's job easier. Helping your boss look good cultivates, more often than not, your boss's support.

- Conduct career reality checks. Seek out peers who can essentially become internal consultants for you. Reciprocate by being their sounding board for new ideas.

- Build support from above and below by volunteering for assignments that will be noticed by other departments across your organization.

- Navigate political land mines by developing strong communication with other women and with potential mentors and allies throughout your organization.

- Reinforce the value of mentoring by becoming one yourself. Mary Rowe, ombudsperson at MIT, recommends viewing mentoring as a reciprocal relationship. "Do whatever you can to help your mentors forever after, and give credit in public for the help you've gotten from them."[5]

- Avoid the trap of learning from a boss or mentor and in the process being cast in a helper role for too long.

- Don't expect a mentor to guide your career forever, nor to learn everything from a single mentor.

- Concentrate on building coalitions to break into the circles where organizational decisions are made. Seize opportunities for constructive feedback, even though the words will not always be easy to hear. Ask your boss, your colleagues, or even an outside consultant to critique your work and your career plan.

- If there are no viable mentors within your organization or through professional associations or if you need only short-term advice, pay for career tune-ups with career coaches or take training programs on presentation and leadership skills.

REVISING THE ORGANIZATION'S UNWRITTEN RULES

"Question: What would you like to say to the head of your organization about removing barriers for women in the workplace?

Answer: How do you expect your daughter to make a living?"
—A Boston management consultant

Although many of the women who responded to my survey work in organizations appearing on the "best companies for women" lists, 62 percent reported experiencing gender inequity in their current positions, defined as "differential or exclusionary treatment in the workplace based solely on gender." Surprisingly, size and type of organization had little impact on how they answered this question. Women working in organizations of under 100 employees were just as likely to report gender bias as women in medium-sized companies and large corporations.

Only 17 percent of the 325 women I surveyed said that gender discrimination does not exist in their organizations. Leading the list of barriers that they believe perpetuate gender inequity "to a great extent" was "the old boys' network" (66 percent), closely followed by "attitudes of senior management" (65 percent). Also high on their list were the "behind-the-scenes rules of work" (51 percent) and "attitudes of middle management" (44 percent). Not surprisingly, 64 percent of the women—all of whom have already broken through middle management—foresee barriers to reaching their future career goals.

These themes echo the results of a 1994 *Working Woman* survey of 500 female executives at the level of vice president or above, in which respondents listed "a male-dominated corporate culture" as the greatest obstacle to success in their companies; "56 percent of the respondents said that they knew female managers who had quit because of the stifling atmosphere."[1] Similarly, a 1996 Catalyst survey of 461 women at the level of vice president or above in Fortune 1000 companies indicated that they were "more than twice as likely as CEOs to consider . . . inhospitable work environments as a barrier to women's advancement."[2] Forty-two percent reported "Male stereotyping and preconceptions of women" as a key factor holding back women's careers; 49 percent cited "exclusion from informal networks" as an advancement barrier.[3]

Where is the infrastructure that sustains this male culture? Clues can be found in the premium placed on face time in the office, in the absence of objective performance standards, and in the business relationship-building to which women are generally not welcome.

Only 5 percent of the senior managers in the country's top industrial and service companies are women. Only two women hold CEO positions in Fortune 1000 companies. And the organizational tone comes from the top. Little seems to have changed since *Business Week* revealed the results of a 1990 survey of 450 women executives. Sixty percent of these women, all in large corporations, reported the male-dominated corporate culture as a roadblock to their success on the job. Twenty percent of these executive women were convinced that their company will never name a woman as CEO; nearly 50 percent believed it would take more than ten years before a woman fills the top job in their organizations.[4]

One woman in upper-middle management in a large manufacturing company commented, "I have worked in three Fortune 200 corporations and two smaller companies. I have found that the prevalence of gender bias is directly related to the behavior of the senior managers. In some cases, this behavior is contradicted by their claimed 'beliefs.' These are the cultures that are the most treacherous." A CPA observed, "Today's discrimination is quiet and disguised. Equal opportunity policies are great, but until attitudes change, as well as the way we do business, the experience for women will not change."

This chapter is quite different in tone and approach from the others because it focuses on the organization rather than the woman. On some levels, it is less optimistic because of the current snail's pace of attitudinal change described by the great majority of women I surveyed. But by identifying the often silent organizational barriers, it offers a blueprint for real change: for men who want to understand and resolve the barriers that persist for half of their talent pool; for women managers and supervisors who want to set an inclusive tone within their departments or divisions; for those with responsibility for human resource management; and for strategic planning committees and in-house women's groups.

American business currently faces a wrenching period of introspection in its efforts to maintain its competitive edge. A leaner, meaner method of managing business has driven away potential for new approaches to managing a diverse workforce. Basic economic survival should dictate that every organization needs the loyalty and commitment of all its available talent. But it has not played out that way for two reasons. First, there is no shortage of employees at the managerial level. Second, many men still resist the acceptance of women as equal colleagues and potential leaders.

Organizations that view gender equity as a legitimate business concern would certainly prefer a quick fix, but they cannot create a new structure that wholeheartedly includes women without first identifying the fundamental flaws in the old ways of conducting business—flaws that trail women from their first job interview to the day they enter the corporate boardroom. Among the women I met, senior executives identified the same barriers to their careers as the women in middle and upper-middle management.

Simply put: Gender equity remains disturbingly absent from the hearts and minds of most senior executives.

Beyond Lip Service: A Message to the CEO

Organizational strategies for gender reform can be undermined by the lens through which business leaders and hiring managers view a woman's professional skills, her potential for leadership, and her career commitment. At times more frustrating than outright discrimination, unspoken attitudes about gender derive their power from their invisibility. Oftentimes, the most formidable barriers that isolate and exclude women in the workplace remain intact and unaddressed.

Most organizations do not recognize—or choose not to recognize—that a problem exists. The formula for eliminating gender exclusion is only self-evident to those who recognize it as a legitimate problem. When I asked, "What would you like to say to the head of your organization about removing barriers for women in the workplace?" woman after woman offered comments like "It would be futile to try," or "He is a model for holding women back even if he doesn't realize it." Emily Powers*, an attorney, advocates bringing the issue to a personal level and suggests, "Think about how you would want your daughter treated and use that as your goal."

Women in every field expressed profound cynicism about the potential even for educating senior management about unresolved gender bias. A Boston banker expressed the frustration I heard from many women: "It's just not worth the discussion. They either get it or they don't." A real estate property manager observed, "The 'good old boys' network precludes some of the most talented people in the organization from getting the recognition they deserve."

Many women expressed the view that they had entered their professions hopeful that this was the generation that would represent a turning point for fair treatment and equal opportunity on the job.

With M.B.A.'s, law degrees, and technical training in hand, many, however, have reached the midpoint of their careers with a very different reality.

One California woman summarized the theme I heard again and again from women who have advanced, taking responsibility themselves for breaking through career roadblocks in their organizations. "Formal programs that have the appearance of supporting women do not hide the fact that we don't have women in senior positions," she says. "The real message is clear."

Frustrated about the inability of business leadership to translate equal opportunity policies into enlightened management practice, a woman in finance commented, "Fifty percent of the new hires have been women for a long time now, but zero percent are partners at the firm. Something's wrong here." A vice president in the insurance industry suggested, "Stop talking about gender equity and start giving women some bold assignments that will allow them to sink or swim just like the boys." One woman working in a brokerage firm said she would like to tell her CEO, "Walk the talk!"

In answer to the question "What do you believe is the best strategy for convincing the leadership of organizations that gender equity is a business concern that affects the bottom line?", many women said they have reluctantly reached the conclusion that class-action suits may be the fastest catalyst for corporate change. A telecommunications marketing director recommends, "Get a few lawsuits going. That's the only thing I've seen get our large company moving." Another woman said, "In a large organization, I honestly believe that there must be a clear and present threat to the purse strings and to corporate public relations." One manager in a large utility company offered the ultimate plan for convincing American business that women's contributions affect the bottom line: "Every woman in the country should stop work for one day."

Many of the women who know they are clearly producing and contributing to the bottom-line goals of their companies, firms, banks, and nonprofits without adequate recognition are quietly researching competitor organizations or are positioning themselves to start their own ventures. Before reaching the decision to get out, most first take a hard look at themselves and ask, "Did I work hard enough? Did I work long enough? Did I do everything in my power to demonstrate my skills and dedication to my career?" Those that are staying are now challenging corporate leaders to consider that same kind of tough and often painful introspection that can reset the tone of an organization and to examine the codes of conduct on which the traditional corporate culture has thrived.

THE IMPACT OF THE UNWRITTEN RULES

A strong factor inhibiting real organizational change is the subtlety attached to certain forms of gender bias that takes place behind doors closed to women. A physician at a university health center comments, "Male supervisors today are aware that they should not verbalize negative statements about women, but they can quietly manipulate the work environment so that men remain in the more powerful positions." An environmental consultant shares this view: "Male senior managers hire clones of themselves." One law partner believes that deeply ingrained male business standards limit the range of styles and behavior that are deemed acceptable for women. "It's risky to be seen as a woman who is too strong or too independent," she says.

A male-dominated corporate culture plays itself out in who is included in informal communication channels, who gets the high-profile assignment, who gets heard in meetings, how ability and potential are evaluated, who is given tips about a client prospect or about developmental opportunities, and whose name is raised in a search committee. Workplace relationships tend to follow lines of personal affiliation, and here, gender often plays a primary role. The male bonding factor can work against a woman in two ways. First, it can be a signal to women that they are still considered "outsiders" at certain levels of their organizations. And second, it can inhibit men from giving women the honest performance feedback they feel comfortable offering to a "buddy."

Because of the small number of senior executive women, only a limited number of studies examine the differences between female and male leaders. One such study, conducted by the Center for Creative Leadership in North Carolina, concluded that "in order to approach the highest levels, women are expected to have more strengths and fewer faults than their male counterparts."[5] Among the 461 female exeutives surveyed in Catalyst's 1996 study, 61 percent rated "developing a style with which male managers are comfortable" as "critical" to their career success—an indication that senior women are still required to fit into a male-dominated culture.[6]

Sixty-eight percent of the women in my sample believe they are held to a higher performance standard than their male colleagues. This belief is fortified not by random and capricious observations but by comparing their cumulative career experiences with those of the men with whom they trained in college, business school, and law school. A disturbing 40 percent of these women do not believe they are paid at the same level as male colleagues with the same credentials. An insurance risk manager describes the double standard's business impact: "It promotes low morale, which spills over into the work product."

According to the unwritten rules of many organizations, perceptions about ability and business contribution may be as important as the reality. Performance standards are, in many cases, less clearly quantifiable at the more senior levels of organizations. In addition, managers are often most comfortable grooming and promoting others cast in their own image of what constitutes career promise and professional success. One woman described the human element that perpetuates the double standard, "It's related to a comfort level with all the other men in senior management, which makes them truly believe that men are 'better' in business."

The easiest solution for eliminating the double standard is, as engineer and M.B.A.-trained manager Glenda Anderson suggests, for every business leader to "frequently pause and ask yourself, 'If this employee were a man, would I handle the situation differently?' Then teach everyone in the organization to ask that same question." And what does the organization gain in return for this corporate soul-searching? What it gains, responds Glenda, is a person who "delivers exceptional results to the organization that lets her thrive."

Ellen James*, a senior manager in the automotive industry, talks of how the two years she spent with a Japanese company were the highlight of her career. "It was like I died and went to heaven." What made this experience so markedly different from her twelve years with a U.S. business was, she says, a different work ethic where "managers are expected to motivate and encourage their people. The Japanese have a very honest, strong respect for people. They clearly define what kind of behavior is acceptable and what kind of behavior is not. And that's the only behavior they tolerate."

Having come from an environment where lewd comments about women were well within the acceptable codes of workplace conduct, this manager felt energized by a genuine team concept, high performance standards, and the company's excellent relationships with suppliers and customers. "What I found so exceptional about the Japanese work culture is how deeply ingrained it is in the way they act every day. No one had to sit me down and explain it to me."

The business relationships that define a work ethic are often solidified in the "schmooze" time that often takes place, for example, over a glass of beer or in a men's locker room. Business conducted on the golf course was a subject that elicited a highly polarized response among my survey group. Some respondents felt that learning to play golf represented a viable option for getting the ear of senior management or the rainmaking clients. More expressed the opinion that after-hours socializing on the golf course deliberately excludes women from the real business action.

"The golf cliché is overdone, but it's also true," suggests Caryn Moir, a product manager at Pacific Bell. In a previous job, Caryn was, at first, pleased to learn that annual salary reviews were done by five managers and their bosses who would meet as a team—that is, until the word got out that the rankings were done on the golf course one Friday afternoon. While the men might argue that the golf course is where they feel relaxed and comfortable without workplace distractions, Caryn cannot help but wonder how objective performance standards are when they are determined after eighteen holes of golf. Putting job-outcome measures on a white board in a conference room and erasing and rewriting rankings once all employees have been discussed is bound to result in a more carefully reasoned outcome. As Caryn points out, "I would have had the same negative reaction if a bunch of women managers had gone out shopping and done the employee salary ratings along the way." But Caryn also offers high praise for a company that learns from missteps like this. "Once this issue was raised, it never happened again. Everyone agreed that what happened was inappropriate." And Caryn adds, "There's always room for growth here and room for change."

Clients often become the excuse for business socializing that excludes women. Emily Powers was surprised when she was not invited to her law firm's marketing event at a local tennis club. "I'm a good tennis player, and I had worked on cases with everyone who was going. So I was really insulted that I was not invited." When Emily asked a colleague why she was omitted from the invitation list, he stammered a bit at first and then admitted, "The client asked that no women attend—not even the senior women from his company. He wanted it to be a guy thing."

WHY ALLEGED SOLUTIONS AREN'T WORKING

The alleged solutions to gender inequity—affirmative action, formalized mentor programs, gender-awareness training, work-family initiatives—at first appeared to be hopeful forerunners of an anticipated milestone in which women would at last achieve equal opportunity. These well-intentioned business initiatives endorsed policies designed to equalize the opportunity scale for women at every level of the workplace. Why, then, are we still talking about unequal treatment for women at work? Because programs and policies that might have been the cornerstones for attitudinal change are often practiced in a piecemeal fashion without integration into long-range planning, with little follow-through, and with virtually no accountability.

In theory, gender awareness training has the potential to be a useful management tool, but without follow-up to support its goals, it can quickly default into a one-time effort. Often resented by those required to attend, even high-quality training is not taken seriously when so many powerful and respected managers convey a different message through their hiring and promotion practices.

Mandated mentoring programs, while formulated under optimistic expectations, may miss the mark when it comes to significant long-term results—unless they are linked to an integrated plan for gender equity. At any level beyond basic information and orientation, mentoring works best when it happens "naturally," under conditions of shared professional interests and a personal chemistry—in which information about political land mines and strategic advice is shared between people who trust one another.

In a study that examined barriers to advancement faced by women in large New York City law firms, one female partner said, "My perception is that most of the mentoring relationships that seem to work don't develop because somebody walks down the hall and says, 'Thou shalt be my mentee,' but because they've been together at two o'clock in the morning getting something done and realize that there's something there."[7]

Mentoring can be helpful for new employees—both women and men. Viewed as a useful orientation tool, entry-level professional and support staff at the Goddard Space Flight Center are assigned mentors outside of their department as part of a formal two-year training program. But formalized mentor programs at more senior levels are unlikely to solve gender access barriers unless they are linked with other strategies to foster the equal treatment of women.

A few companies, in an effort to move women up the career ladder in more representative numbers, have endorsed the controversial strategy of linking a percentage of their managers' bonuses to their record in promoting employees from underrepresented groups. While this strategy can be useful in prompting managers to consider a broader candidate pool for each job search, its weakness lies in the perception that tokenism will prevail.

Tokenism represents an organizational trap dangerous to gender equity and one more excuse not to tackle the real change required. It benefits no one and denigrates the talents of women who deserve to advance. Women are not looking for special treatment because of their gender. They simply seek a fair shake at advancement, skill and talent recognition, and compensation.

Abigail Beutler, an early trailblazer in the automotive industry and now retired, talks about the danger that misdirected corporate motives pose for women's advancement. "Sometimes, in the name of gender equity, corporations advance women to levels beyond reasonable expectations for success. Then they can say, 'See, we did it, but the woman failed.' And the failure of one woman is generalized to include all women. That puts undue pressure on the rising woman who recognizes that the future of many women in her organization depends on her."

Karen Poniatowski, a program manager at the National Aeronautics and Space Administration (NASA), cautions, "Remove any employee—male or female—who is not performing. When you hire women and minorities in visible positions, be sure it is done fairly and that the people are qualified. Don't perpetuate stereotypes by hiring and keeping on unqualified women and minorities."

Having been "the first woman" in several of her jobs at NASA, Karen recognizes that removing gender barriers "is painful work to do right. Culture change takes patience and consistency—not found in a firefighting, downsizing environment." Recognizing that civil service guidelines protect white males with seniority, she is concerned that downsizing becomes yet another excuse to put off gender reform at work. The slow pace of change in her own organization of 24,000 employees is demonstrated by the thirty-two women who have reached senior management, representing just 5 percent of the upper ranks.

The ready excuse for the startling discrepancy between the retention and advancement rates for men and women has been that women derail their own careers by taking time off to have children. The reality is that most women return to work after a parental leave and those who believe they are treated well by their organizations return sooner than those who are treated poorly. When the Big Six accounting firm Deloitte & Touche examined the unusually high turnover rate among its women employees, it had assumed that family reasons accounted for this trend. Instead, 90 percent left the firm to take other jobs. Among the small number of mothers at home, most planned to return to work.[8]

While putting into place progressive polices to support family needs certainly supports the retention of valuable employees for a relatively brief period in their careers, they do little to counteract gender bias over the life of a career. A 1995 survey of managers in companies with established work-family programs revealed that 70 percent of the managers believe there is a glass ceiling at their companies.[9]

LEADERSHIP BY EXAMPLE

The tone of every organization is filtered through the business outlook, the professional standards, and the values held by its leaders. How women are treated begins with the examples set by those who head up organizations.

China Gorman, a group vice president for Drake, Beam, and Morin, says that "when those who hold the purse strings realize that people from all groups affect the bottom line, change will happen." She applauds the leadership of her organization for its gender-blind recognition of business talent, in which four of the six operating managers are women. But recognizing that corporate responsibility for social change extends beyond the walls of her building, she challenges progressive business leaders to assume a higher profile in the corporate community to confront and resolve gender inequality.

The selection process for leadership nurtures an environment in which a comfortable choice can take precedence over a talented person who does not fit the traditional corporate mold. More than 95 percent of senior executives are men and within this group, 97 percent are white men. Asked what she would say to her CEO about removing barriers to women's careers, one woman replied, "He doesn't realize he perpetuates many of them by his words and his behavior. And that discourages many of the female 'rising stars' who eventually leave and join our competitors."

Those who challenge a work environment that's not supportive of women may, sadly, place more barriers in their own career path. Frances Conley, M.D., candidly admits that she made the difficult choice to be the whistle-blower on a known harasser about to accept a leadership position in her department at Stanford University Medical School. Despite her superb credentials as a neurosurgeon, a researcher, and a manager with business school training, she is blacklisted forever from a leadership slot at Stanford (see Chapter 6).

Now as head of the local Veterans Administration clinic, Frances has made it her personal mission to demonstrate new models for leadership. In "her" organization, Frances diligently creates a shared sense of purpose among all employees—at every level of the organization. As she strives to change the work culture in terms of "human-to-human contact," she emphasizes the value contributed by every member of her team. Frances insists upon a tone of mutual respect, a key, she believes, to preventing a hostile work environment.

Although many organizations tout their commitment to the noble concept of egalitarian team-building, few act on it. Frances practices what she preaches. She has carefully set the tone of her leadership by daily example. New residents are welcomed by a speech that begins: "This is the way the game is played here, and it's different from other hospitals. We respect each other. We like each other. My secretary is an equally important part of my team—as are the nurses."

Frances's bottom-line goal is patient care. The end result of her careful team-building is better patient care provided by a committed staff whose high morale means low turnover. In addition, she has noticed a reduction in her recruitment and training costs. Equally applicable to a traditional business setting, Frances's credibility as a leader is founded on a generous sharing of credit with her entire team, where respect is not based on gender or hierarchy of position but on the value of collaboration.

Anyone with supervisory responsibilities can use their leadership to rewrite the traditional rules of work. Joanna Engelke, a vice president at Bain & Company, a management consulting firm, describes her approach to managing work teams. "My goal is to take the little zone I'm responsible for—the group of people I have some influence over—and change the ground rules for how work gets done," she explains. Since Joanna prefers to be home with her family most evenings, one of her managerial goals has been to figure out how to get the work done efficiently. And she told her last team, "In order not to work nights and weekends, we have to be much smarter up front about planning and figuring out the resources we need to get this project done on time. We're all going to have to commit to doing exactly what we say we're going to do."

There are people at Bain & Company who love working for Joanna. But changing the rules carries some risk. As Joanna has found, "There's another crowd that thinks you're not really making it, you're not on the hottest, hippest team unless you're here every night and every weekend—even when the work could get done during daylight hours."

Leadership by Design

With great humor, Joanna Engelke describes how knowledge about macho pastimes has helped her male colleagues promote their business expertise. In one case, Joanna was waiting in a client's office with another consultant, ready to make their first pitch. "We wanted to make a good impression. There were these stuffed animal heads all over the office, and my peer from Bain was savvy enough to recognize that they were not deer but were elk or something. So he didn't make the mistake of saying something about deer when our client walked in." As luck would have it, her colleague had been canoeing the weekend before where there was nothing to read except an outdoor magazine about bow hunting. "He just happened to read it and was able to name-drop bow hunting terminology with the client," Joanna recalls. "And he got the job. Now maybe I could have gotten the job too, but no way could I ever duplicate that story!"

The predominant and visible male symbolism that enshrouds most organizations is yet another reminder of a woman's intrusionary status. How many wood-paneled conference rooms are adorned with portraits of the organization's male executives or more recent photographs of male golf outings? These symbols would seem petty were it not for the fact that these corporate messages reflect and reinforce a limited vision of who should lead the organization.

Assistant United States Attorney Elizabeth Woodcock points to the challenges of a "male-sized" courtroom where the podium is designed for a tall male, a minor detail were it not for the "maleness" that affects many aspects of her days on the job. Elizabeth acknowledges that while many experienced male lawyers have been mentors to her, she has never had a female mentor. "The federal defense bar in Maine is still dominated by men. When I was a law clerk, both of the judges for whom I clerked were men. I have tried more than a dozen cases in the last four years, but I have been opposed by a woman only twice.

There are no female magistrates or judges in Maine's federal courts, so I have no female role models there."

HOW WE SELECT LEADERS

Setting the tone for gender equity does not require the exclusion of talented men, but it does broaden the criteria for leadership. Many executive women described the one-dimensional characteristics exhibited by the people selected to lead organizations. Frances Conley believes, "We're not choosing leadership correctly. We're still looking for the heroic manager. We're looking for the person who spends 23 out of 24 hours of every day on the job, including Saturday and Sunday, and who does not have the time or compassion for a family life."

When Frances is asked to participate in a leadership search, she interviews the clerical staff and the nurses. Her male colleagues ask her, wide-eyed, "Why would you want to meet with them?" She does it because she can take from these groups a more accurate pulse of the workplace climate and morale and from this an understanding of the criteria needed for the person selected. "When I spend an hour or two with the staff, I usually find out about people who treat them with respect, who respect the job they do, who make sure that they are valued. It's that kind of person I want as a leader. I want somebody who treats people fairly—who has enough 'ego strength' of their own to reach out a hand and help other people advance." She is convinced that the ideal search process involves checking references from the bottom up as well as the top down. Her rationale? "I want to see people who build other people. I want people who are passionate about making the careers of other people happen."

Associate Professor Irena Makarushka views her presence on search committees as a golden opportunity to change the standards set when only men apply for the jobs. To offset the rigid expectations for traditional male career paths, Irena challenges the assumptions behind them—assumptions that often lead to dismissive judgments about a woman's work history. Irena has noticed in case after case that while search committees rarely question a brief hiatus on a man's curriculum vitae, for a woman they are quick to point out, "There seems to be a gap in her publishing. This concerns me." Irena's unspoken response is, "Well, of course, there's a short-term gap. So what? She has three children under the age of 3." Instead, Irena suggests that the committee look at her current and future potential, asking, "Does taking a parental leave make her a bad person or an incompetent educator? How can we interpret this not negatively but in the context of the person's larger life?"

Moving Women to the Top

The Sisters of Charity Healthcare System in Houston, Texas, a Catholic health-care system comprised of hospitals, long-term health-care centers, physician clinics, and health maintenance organizations in four states, recently announced Opportunity 2000—an aggressive and comprehensive approach to succession planning.

The program was designed, through the sponsorship of the Congregation of the Sisters of Charity of the Incarnate Word, as one response to the active commitment of senior leadership to cultural and gender diversity. The System recognized its own "glass ceiling" and to counteract the effects, Opportunity 2000 was set up as a fast-track executive development program for women.

The program relies on women creating their own development plan, in collaboration with their bosses, to identify gaps in specific management experiences, in areas that might include mergers and acquisitions, reorganization projects, or working with governing boards. Developmental goals are met through special assignments; cross functional team leadership; business and leadership education and training; partnering with top management in their organizations; and mentoring support.

This carefully conceived program evolved from Women in Partnership, a pilot program for women in hospital administration who wanted to move into management. Gayle Capozzalo, SCH senior vice president of organizational development and chair of the Opportunity 2000 board, is clear about the program's mission. "This is a program to ensure that we have qualified women in the pipeline for executive management openings," she says. "This is not an anti-male program; we just want to be sure that we are using the strengths of both genders."

"To address the inequities for women that have evolved in the executive arena,"[10] Opportunity 2000 follows this model:

- A careful screening process. From an initial informational session attended by more than 200 women in the hospital network, sixty-two submitted applications. Thirty-two were invited to attend a 1½ day career evaluation workshop, out of which twenty-seven chose to continue the application process. Seven final participants were selected for the first group in the program.

- A clear time frame for meeting developmental goals in three years. New participants will enter the program about every two years. Applicants must have at least ten years left before they expect to retire.

- A careful matching of mentors with participants, based on participants' developmental plans and the advice of their boss, CEO, and Managing Board adviser.

- Accountability for each participant through semiannual benchmarking of progress.

- An honest recognition that men may feel threatened by this program and reassurance from top management that men will not automatically be passed over for promotions.

- A realistic goal of moving two women into CEO positions by the year 2000 and a broader goal of encouraging other women who want to enter leadership positions.

President and CEO Stan Urban says, "By providing Opportunity 2000, the Sisters of Charity Healthcare System is actively living out its commitment to cultural and gender diversity. We see this as an ongoing process, and we are committed to it. The entire system will benefit as we draw on the talents and strengths of both genders to create our future."

REVISING THE UNWRITTEN RULES

An article that addressed the resistance in many organizations to inclusive management offered the following conclusion: "Does all the tension between men and women sound grossly overstated? Hardly. The fact is, gender relations in the workplace are worse than they've ever been because we've patently ignored the real reasons behind gender warfare: Women want more power, and men don't want to share it . . ." [11] The assumption that "when one side wins, the other misses out on something" can limit, and even sabotage, the achievements of women as they progress through the managerial pipeline.

When asked what she would like to say to business leaders about removing barriers for women, Pacific Bell's Caryn Moir suggested, "Suspend your perception of the corporate culture." Realistically, Caryn acknowledges that gender equity is not a concept you can just "cram down their throats." Caryn's approach to changing the rules of work while remaining a member of the team is predicated on viewing men as potential allies who need to first find common ground. For women and men who work side by side, finding common ground admittedly requires both patience and persistence.

Because most business relationships are predicated on examples and standards set by men, women often walk a fine line between knowing which battles to fight and which to just give in to. Making themselves "fit in" through accommodation, say many executive women, has allowed them to survive but has failed to address the behind-the-scenes rules of work still more likely to benefit a man more than a woman with the same business expertise.

Women, themselves, cannot control all of the intangible elements surrounding access to equal opportunity. Lynne Slater, equal opportunity manager for the Goddard Space Flight Center, recalls an engineer who returned from a national conference where she went to dinner with four other women in her field. In telling this story, Lynne described the fundamental benefit of, for once, not being "the only woman": "This had never happened before. The conversation was just so different. I didn't know what I had been missing. And communication was going on at so many different levels."

Prompted by this and similar conversations with other women about the pitfalls of career isolation, Lynne now sets up forums where women meet their counterparts from other divisions. One of these is a two-day, value-based decision-making class where "women who participated in this class several years ago have been getting together ever since. And that sets up one network for them." Wary that these networks among women heighten isolation from the men in the office, Lynne also encourages women to seek out male mentors. "There's a lot they can learn from the men here. As long as they establish some boundaries in the relationship, it works fine."

Pressure to adapt to the norms that fortify the traditional rules of work, suggests Lynne, is transmitted "a thousand different ways." Having observed that many of the women selected for the government's senior executive service are essentially isolated from other women because of pressure to conform, they have, she says, "adopted the white-male value system." One senior woman, a highly respected scientist, was told by her boss not to help women so much because it would damage her career. Soon after this, she left the program and the government lost a talented woman.

Lynne has also noticed a new resistance to adherence to the 10–12 hour work day. Employees who rejected that work ethic are not considered to be serious about their careers. Now young women and young men, committed to both their work and a personal life, close her office door and tell her, "We're not doing that."

To many of this generation, the limited merits of face time as the standard for career commitment are obvious: Is the person who, year after year, works a 12-hour day always the most productive? Do some of these people socialize a lot or take long lunches? What happens to the parent—male or female—who leaves the office in time to be home for dinner but regularly opens a full briefcase after the children are asleep?

THE LAST FRONTIER: ATTITUDES

Attitudinal change is the final and most critical frontier yet to be won. The basic principles of good management practice—missing in many organizations—are the cornerstones to an inclusionary workplace where the best talent rises, regardless of gender or any other personal characteristics. One partner in a management consulting firm suggests that "it's costly to waste investment in people who don't advance. We're growing too fast to find the best talent only in men." When a woman walks through the door of an organization, what is in place to ensure that her talent and contribution will not be shunted by workplace barriers to gender equity? What are the lessons to be learned from organizations that enable both genders to become fully valued, contributing, productive members of the workplace?

Lynne Slater suggests that organizations need to develop the values that society traditionally associates with women: values centered on human relationships; value placed on home and family. This shift, she believes, would benefit the health of employees as well as the longevity of the organization. "Well-balanced people tend to be more productive. They make better and more creative decisions," she points out. "So much of the male-dominated organization is predicated on immediate results, and that just burns people out." Realistic about the challenge ahead for those who seek to transform the culture of work, Lynne says, "It's going to be really hard to make changes with all the emphasis on better, faster, cheaper, and leaner and meaner. But to preserve itself, the organization needs to take time to integrate some of these other values."

To demonstrate the bottom-line imperative for changing the culture, Lynne quantifies the information that supports her case for reform. Rather than simply stating that which she knows to be true—that highly qualified women are often passed over for advancement opportunities—Lynne uses numbers to make her point. "We've done some studies on performance ratings. I have found that, on average, women are rated higher than men in each of our major occupational groups and at each grade level," she says. "That starts a dialogue about why women's careers aren't progressing as fast as men's."

Lynne provides senior management with data on gender, packaged in a way that will cause an "Aha! I get it!" reaction. She says, "I work with scientists and engineers who tend to be curious. So they want to test the things we tell them. They ask their wives. They start to watch what's going on around them. When they're challenged, they look for data." With humor, Lynne admits, "Often they are looking for data to disprove me, but since I'm not usually wrong, they can't disprove it."

With ten years of organizational credibility behind her, Lynne is now in a position where she can count on the backing of top management when she needs to resolve the issues raised by women. One reward for her longevity comes from the fact that some of the people who she helped early in their careers are now in senior positions. "I have been educating them along the way."

Change has not come overnight, and Lynne is the first to admit that even her organization has a long reach toward total gender equity. She keeps close tabs on the equal-opportunity tone of the Goddard Space Flight Center by holding focus groups for each employee group, in which women from each division sit down for lunch with senior management. Meeting with the women in advance of these sessions allows Lynne to brainstorm with the group and to prioritize the obstacles they want to address.

THE VISIONARY ORGANIZATION

While it's easy to pass the burden of responsibility for gender equity onto "the organization," companies can only be as progressive as the people who work in them. Many managers and business leaders remain stuck in some bad habits. Opening up career paths to a broader range of talent, objectifying performance systems, and developing effective teams will benefit both women and the corporation.

Sound and consistent personnel management remedies gender inequity, but such practice is, in reality, the exception. In most organizations, the human resource function is accorded low respect and limited resources. When creatively managed, strategic planning for an organization's employee base benefits both women and men.

What can an organization do to begin to reverse the daily manifestations of a work environment that is comfortably and quietly subversive to a woman's career?

- Invest time in a performance management system that allows each employee to rise to his or her productive potential. Having multiple reviewers in an employee's annual review is one option for a team approach to setting standards and providing checks and balances that objectively analyze one's results and potential.

- Conduct career opportunity audits that examine comparative promotion and retention rates between women and men who enter the organization with parallel education and training. Look at performance ratings to separate employees whose weak performance may skew the analysis. Test the reality: Do men rise through the pipeline faster than equally or more-talented women?

- Look at overall comparative numbers for men and women in whom the organization has invested resources for professional development (conferences, professional associations, training seminars, executive education programs). If these numbers suggest that the organization is doing a good job at unbiased access to career opportunities, use this information to your business advantage. Communicate it in recruitment and orientation brochures. If, on the other hand, gender appears to be the primary factor in determining who has options for skill enhancement and career visibility, develop a plan that holds individual managers responsible for identifying and supporting high-potential performers regardless of gender.

- Include men in the process of examining and revising the elusive factors that influence promotion: gender-based stereotypes about ability, ambition, and potential; an absence of female role models (and its impact on both women and men); a void in objective performance standards; exclusion of women from informal professional networks.

- Take a courageous look at workplace standards predicated on male-only traditions. The first question to ask is: Are these business traditions really necessary? Informal business networks, mentoring opportunities for those who look and act just like traditional leadership, and after-hours client socializing are among the most firmly entrenched traditions. Critical to career momentum, these informal channels for relationship-building and business communication are fully accessible to most men but quietly unwelcoming to most women.

- Identify high-potential women early in their careers to ensure that they have the same access to career-enhancing opportunities as their male peers: line positions, skill-building opportunities, special-project assignment, appointment to high visibility business teams, and committee and project leadership. Until workplace standards become gender-blind, support nontraditional forums for a woman's career development: sponsorship in community organizations, nomination to business and nonprofit boards, membership in women's business groups. These affiliations help the business by broadening the client base and benefit the woman by connecting her with peers from other organizations as well as with women who are role models and potential mentors.

- Propose and practice new standards for client entertainment. Lunch meetings can be just as effective as the evening beer with a client or vendor.

- Give human resource departments the clout and credibility such workplace changes warrant. Appoint human resource managers whose focus is strategic planning, performance management, employee reward and recognition, and succession planning.

- Conduct job searches that are truly open. Too many senior positions are quietly reserved for a white male candidate even before they are announced, sending a message that may cause women to self-select out of the process. Staff search committees with people who will identify the broadest possible candidate base, uncovering nontraditional sources for nominees via community groups, nonprofit boards, and professional organizations whose membership represents today's labor pool.

- Offer managers a "tool kit" for change with a range of options for first educating staff on the barriers that persist for women and then for addressing the issues in a problem-solving way. Strategies for understanding and prioritizing the issues include confidential focus groups, workplace climate surveys, and training on specific issues such as sexual harassment.

- Hold supervisors responsible for meeting the goals set by your organization's plan for gender equity. Linking a manager's compensation to a quota system is not the way to go. But a manager, for example, should be rewarded for fostering a climate where women flood the applicant pools and move up the ranks at the same rate as their male peers. Or a department head might receive recognition for effectively piloting alternative work options.

- Adopt interim measures to promote what may be, in many organizations, painful and unwilling gender reform. In-house women's groups, if sanctioned and supported by the top, can help demonstrate the link between gender equity and the bottom line. An ombudsperson reporting directly to a senior executive can meet the need for in-house mediation on bias incidents and sexual harassment allegations, while serving as an educator and advocate for organizational change.

- Address work-family issues from the perspective of their impact on recruitment and retention. What happens to the careers of people who use "family-friendly" policies and benefits? Is it viewed as a burden to accommodate a parental leave? Are parents treated as second-class citizens upon their return from a leave? Do part-timers stay with the company or seek employment elsewhere?

- Schedule confidential exit interviews with women who leave your organization, ideally with an ombudsperson or someone outside the company. Analyze the interview results. Take a close look at the experiential differences in the daily lives of women and men who work side by side. If the differences account for men enjoying a gender advantage, develop a business plan for gender equity, with measurable goals and accountability for their implementation.

- Send a message from the top of the organization, which signals a new business agenda where women enjoy the freedom to make unencumbered career decisions, where the organization accepts a broader range of leadership styles, and where the very best talent rises.

CHAPTER 12

INVENTING YOUR OWN AGENDA

"The world is changing. The female manager of the future won't have to be a hard-driving, workaholic, make-believe good old boy to be successful."

— Ellen Gaucher, senior associate director,
University of Michigan Hospitals[1]

All of the women I interviewed exhibited the courage to be themselves. They do not identify with any one managerial style, but many practice a common set of strategies to clear the path for a gender-blind career. Each has the confidence to maintain her own sense of values in the process of achieving career success. She is ambitious and not afraid to admit it. She is not threatened by the success of other women and, in fact, extends a helping hand to women inside her organization and in the broader business community. She is willing to take unpopular stands when that is what is needed to get a job done. She does not allow herself to be demoralized by men who cannot accept her as an equal. She recognizes that the men in her office may be more threatened by the change women represent for their organizations than by the women themselves.

None of the women is so foolishly idealistic as to expect that she can immediately break through every gender barrier faced on the job. Yet, optimism that she can influence change, coupled with the reward she finds in her work, inspires her to look forward. There is no room for guilt or feelings of victimization. Both are a waste of precious energy that she would prefer to save for her life outside the office.

The new managerial woman is:

- An educator and change agent

- A realist

- A risk-taker

- A pragmatist

- An alliance builder

- A role model

- A visionary

All are fully comfortable with high ambition and with their ability to use power and to influence their organizations. None takes herself so seriously that she is unable to laugh at herself as well as at the absurdity that sometimes exists in her organization.

THE EDUCATOR AND CHANGE AGENT

The traditional vantage point on issues about work and gender has been to "help" women fit in rather than to examine the merit of the standards required for the fit. It is no longer enough for managerial women to simply survive a work environment that treats them as outsiders or interlopers.

One or two women in my survey of 325 suggested that if we simply stop talking about gender inequity, the problem will go away as more women prove themselves on the job. But the vast majority disagree. Professor Irena Makarushka takes some of the heat out of discussions about gender equity with this premise: "We all have a point of view. We can challenge one another. We can discuss it. But it's there whether or not we talk about it. To assume that organizations are value-neutral is absurd."

When managerial men are firmly established in a white male power base, how do you convince them that they are not losing something by opening up business opportunities for women? The answer, suggests product manager Caryn Moir, is "You can't. But you can help them understand by showing them what it's like to have the shoe on the other foot—to be an outsider looking in. Male-bashing has always been a problem for me because it's making fun of a stereotype."

Caryn tries to find common ground with male colleagues and superiors, focusing on the contributions women make to the profitability of Pacific Bell, including insight into the needs of one half of the company's customer base. To get out of the "white, male, and worried"[2] trap, Caryn says, "I try to help people understand that just because you have great men out there, that's no reason not to look at all the qualified people in the labor pool. Expanding the size of the pool from which you're hiring increases your opportunities for hiring real quality."

The first step in navigating a workplace still littered with career land mines for women is to understand the male history and traditions on which current practice is solidly grounded. Recognizing that women are not always the intended target of eccentric corporate traditions and that what is hostile to our value system may be repugnant to some men as well, keeps women from needlessly beating their heads against an unyielding wall of exclusion.

To loosen the rigidity typical of most work cultures, the new managerial woman has assumed the role of mediator between men and women and between herself and her organization. When her boss forgets to offer her feedback on her last case or most recent presentation, she approaches him directly. Careful about the tone of her approach, she frames her request for feedback and advice strategically, sending the signal that she is not afraid of criticism and that she is committed to professional growth. When she initiates the use of new workplace practices, such as an alternative work schedule, she presents her boss with a written plan rather than a managerial problem.

THE REALIST

Learning to separate who we are from what we do has helped many women take some of the personal sting out of gender bias. Even under the worst of circumstances, this removes the option of giving into defeat. Rather than believing "if my male colleagues can't accept me on the team, I must be doing something wrong," today's manager knows she is not in the wrong, she is not responsible for gender bias.

This new attitude enables women to take risks on the job: You win some; you lose some. You're not a failure as a person if your career goes offtrack. The only failing is in not looking for the next opportunity where you can move on and put to use what you have learned from your experiences.

When a work situation becomes intolerable, the realist takes charge of the situation and concludes, "Gender discrimination is so deeply entrenched in this organization that nothing short of a miracle will effect change. Internalizing this frustration and anger will only hurt me." She will vote with her feet as soon as she can strategically position herself to move to another department or leave the organization entirely.

Being a realist also means examining some painful truths about the career traps we may unwittingly push ourselves into: the caretaker-of-the-details trap; the "I need to be all things to all people" trap; the self-blame downward spiral. We must assume responsibility for any self-defeating attitudes we may have.

THE RISK-TAKER

Taking chances on the job exerts more control, not less, over a career. From taking risks in business conversations to taking the job nobody wants to being the bystander who witnesses and stops harassment, the women I met have translated risk into opportunity.

A man can often rely on an institutional buffer zone to protect him from risky assignments that do not go as planned. A woman must rely primarily on her own stamina and sense of self-worth. For a man, a trusted senior manager might offer a hand to get his project back on track. Or he may simply be labeled a self-starter who's a good long-term investment for the company, despite a brief stumble. For a woman, recovery from a career setback often requires proving herself all over again with closer scrutiny and more skepticism than ever about her potential. Only when her high-risk venture succeeds is she deemed an organizational player.

When others attach risk to gender itself, a woman can take great pride in proving them wrong. She finds confidence from within herself. Although most people, if they are candid, will admit to at least some fear of failure, the effective woman keeps any such worry in perspective. In tackling the high-risk/high-reward assignment, she may ask herself, "What's my next move if this strategy doesn't work out?" Her primary goal is to position the risky venture in the context of how it can yield important business results.

A few extraordinary women have assumed the ultimate risk—putting their own careers on the line—to blow the whistle on discrimination or sexual harassment. Women like Stanford Medical School's Frances Conley and the Navy's Paula Coughlin took a stand against work environments blatantly hostile and disrespectful to many women. Each paid a price, losing serious ground in her own career, yet summoning the courage to remove barriers for the women who will follow.

THE PRAGMATIST

The emerging woman leader always positions her professional value in the context of her contribution to the bottom line. But she does not believe in winning at any cost. The end result is important but so are the means of getting there. How she effects change becomes an important model for broadening the range of standards and behavior accepted as credible within organizations.

She has adopted a long-term view on her career. She will make some mistakes, she will work in some impossible situations, she may face harassment. But the new manager will not allow these obstacles to derail her career for the long-term.

Sarah Curran*, a vice president at a large manufacturing firm, points to the danger in too much second-guessing. "I'm always analyzing the last situation and asking myself, 'Could I have done that better?' I'm still my own worst critic, but I have finally realized that my conscience is my best guide, and I know if I really didn't do something right for the business."

Women who have moved through middle management have learned that their way of conducting business may be viewed as less effective simply because it is different from the men down the hall. For example, in watching how male colleagues interact with one another and with clients, the women in my survey observed a marked gender difference in how relationships are built. Wall Street's Marianne Bye characterizes the difference as using information versus deploying muscle. Men often use position, power, and the credibility of their institutions to establish their own business reputation. Women are more likely to rely on client service and the quality of their advice to establish professional worth.

Determination and tenacity are the driving forces behind women making change. Engineer Carol Reukauf advises younger women, "Find a job where you can target people who are going to be powerful and influential. Start volunteering for committees, teams, and interdepartmental projects where you can gain visibility and build alliances."

If one point of access to clients, committees, and board appointments does not pan out, she will find professional recognition with a different strategy. When the options are few for building her credibility from within her organization, she steps outside to develop and showcase her skills on professional boards, community organizations, and women's networks.

When she reaches senior management, she seizes the opportunity to present her vision to the CEO or president. She presents the indisputable facts about the untapped value women hold for American business. At First Boston Corporation, for example, a group of senior women captured the attention of top management with bottom-line numbers showing women, even in dramatically underrepresented numbers, to be among the firm's top revenue producers. The result was a comprehensive business plan to recruit and retain talented women.

At the Goddard Space Flight Center, Lynne Slater presented a technical group of managers with graphs, charts, and overheads showing that time after time, women with top performance ratings are not promoted at the same pace as the men. These managers are now working with Lynne to ensure that the best employees are recognized, regardless of gender.

The ultimate goal of the women I met is to achieve the backing of their organization and genuine acceptance from their male colleagues.

The Alliance-Builder

What you will not see in the résumés of the women I surveyed is a list of their superb skills at building coalitions and facilitating connections among other women. Because they have limited options for advice and sponsorship from above, the new managerial women promote and practice peer mentoring. Women are actively helping one another by delivering feedback on business strategy, providing a confidential sounding board for difficult situations and introducing one another to important business contacts.

The alliance-builder no longer fits the stereotype of the lonely trailblazer: the cold, friendless female worker who, by sheer virtue of her intelligence and drive, pushes forward her business agenda. Instead, she recognizes, realistically, that most successful people have had some help somewhere along the way. Going it alone will be a solitary, less productive road.

Middle and senior management members of California's Pacific Bell women's group have helped women at all levels of the organization find recourse for harassment and remedy for bias on the job. In the Boston area, a group of women in nonprofit organizations offer a hot line to assist others in negotiating compensation for a new job.

Women are also experimenting with new models for effective relationship-building and communication with the men in their office, recognizing that business referrals and mentoring opportunities should not be divided by gender.

THE ROLE MODEL

As they model new standards for effective management and leadership practice, the women I met are setting new examples for women and success.

Pitney Bowes' division president Anne Pol invests in her staff—both women and men—and views their career development as an important management function. Morale and productivity are high in Anne's division, and other departments see that advancing more women into leadership positions is not such a bad thing.

When Susan Galler sits next to trustee Carol Goldberg, a mentor and friend, at a board meeting for Beth Israel Hospital, she watches with admiration how Carol uses humor, directness, and a quick business mind to be recognized and heard in a room filled with men.

For her students, chemist Cynthia Friend models a new style of collaborative learning that encourages team-building rather than competition in the classroom. At another level, she actively lobbies the president of her institution for programs that will retain the best and the brightest, who need occasional scheduling flexibility to meet family needs. Cynthia is nationally recognized in a life-size cardboard likeness that greets entrants to an exhibit at the Smithsonian's Museum of American History. Her image right at the door sends a powerful message about women's professional potential to the next generation of scientists.

As law firm partner Catherine Lee sits on a panel discussion with other lawyers, they openly discuss the challenges of working and parenting. The young women in the audience recognize that the concept of superwoman exists only in fantasy. And they leave the session knowing that although work-family balance is not always perfect, women are helping one another find new answers.

THE VISIONARY

Carol Goldberg offers this advice to business policy setters: "First, focus on workplace barriers that affect all employees. Then, focus on underrepresented groups in the pipeline—from the bottom right up to the top."

Women know that many men may not even be aware that their behavior shuts women out of informal communication networks, management feedback, and opportunities to take risks. And so they are taking it upon themselves to promote an atmosphere of mutual respect and a shared sense of purpose within their organizations. Their vision inspires other women to assert their influence in organizational change.

Fidelity Investments' Debbie Malins describes the components to the confidence she has developed for her business success and her personal vision: "You have to be comfortable with yourself before you can make people comfortable with you. You have to be willing to take risks. You need to step forward with your vision. If one idea gets knocked down, you have to come back with another one. And keep trying until you find ways to make a difference in your organization."

YOUR OWN AGENDA

With a secure confidence in their ability to contribute to the workplace and to the broader society, an emerging group of women leaders offers these practical strategies for clearing the path for equal opportunity on the job. Let each of us learn from them as we set our own agendas:

- Gain control of your own career by taking responsibility for overturning the gender barriers placed in your advancement path.

- Focus on a strategy for making a difference in your organization rather than on the unfairness of its unwritten rules. Refuse to allow justifiable anger and frustration to weigh down the pace of your career.

- When you want to do something contrary to long-standing business practice, make it impossible for your organization to turn you down. Answer all the difficult issues up front, with a well-planned proposal, be it for your four-day work week or to work from home occasionally.

- Keep your eye on your ultimate goal. Adopt a long-term view on altering the minds and attitudes of those still threatened by the changes women are bringing to the workplace.

- Trust your business instincts. As a trailblazer for other women, some of the business territory is still rough going, and your efforts may not always yield immediate results.

- Choose your battles carefully. Confronting every gender-based challenge reduces your personal currency and your chance at overturning the major barriers. Cut your losses when a job situation holds no hope for change.

- Go after the business problem that everyone wants solved but that no one dares assume. This type of initiative brings attention to your skills and showcases your potential to do more.

- Invest in yourself and invest in other women. Alliances among women have become a powerful and productive business force.

- Behave as though you've already won. Successful women have discovered the confidence and the value in being themselves.

SURVEY RESULTS

Breaking Through the Gender Barriers
A National Survey of 325 Professional Women[a]

Summary of Results

DEMOGRAPHICS

Level of Position		Size of Organization		Education	
Middle Management	26%	100 or less	18%	M.B.A.	29%
Upper-Middle Management	29%	101–500	21%	M.A. or M.S	20%
Senior Management	25%	501–2,000	16%	J.D.	18%
Other	20%	2,001+	45%	M.D. or Ph.D.	9%

Marital Status		Age Groups		Do you have children?	
Single, never married	18%	25–34	17%	Yes	60%
Single, divorced	12%	35–44	54%	No	40%
Married	65%	45–54	24%		
Unmarried partnership	5%	55–64	4%	**Number of Children**	
Widowed	.6%	64+	.6%	1	32%
				2	49%
				3	15%
				4+	4%

OPINIONS

Which of the following do you believe perpetuate gender inequity[b]?

	To a Great Extent	To Some Extent	Not at All
Attitudes of senior management	65%	30%	4%
Attitudes of middle management	44%	49%	8%
Attitudes of male colleagues	43%	49%	8%
The behind-the-scenes rules of work	51%	39%	10%
A lack of objective performance standards	27%	44%	29%
Negative stereotypes about women's abilities	28%	49%	23%
A fundamental discomfort with women's multiple roles	35%	53%	12%
A difference in male/female communication styles	42%	51%	7%
The old boys' network	66%	30%	3%
Exclusion of women from after-hours socializing	27%	50%	23%
Absence of female role models	40%	50%	10%
Absence of flexibility for family needs	41%	49%	10%

Has being a woman ever limited your potential in any of the following areas?

	Percentage Who Responded Yes
Compensation	68%
Promotion	67%
Opportunity to have a mentor	57%
Opportunity to take on high-visibility assignments	54%
Opportunity to take career risks	52%
Access to clients/customers	43%
Knowing about open positions	41%
Leadership on committees	39%
Consideration for jobs that require relocation	33%
Leadership in professional organizations	26%

Opinions on the following statements:

	Strongly Agree	Agree Somewhat	Disagree Somewhat	Strongly Disagree
I am paid at the same level as my male colleagues with the same credentials.	27%	33%	24%	16%
I have advanced at the same rate as my male colleagues with the same credentials.	22%	32%	27%	19%
I am held to a higher performance standard than my male colleagues.	24%	44%	20%	12%
Women are expected to take care of the office details, while men are given the plum assignments.	14%	37%	33%	16%
Successful women must make greater personal sacrifices than successful men.	51%	38%	8%	3%
Once a woman has a child, she is automatically perceived to be less committed to her career.	29%	44%	22%	5%

Responses to the following questions:

	Yes	No
In your current position, have you ever experienced gender inequity on the job?	62%	38%
In your current position, have you experienced language that is demeaning to women?	69%	31%
Have you ever experienced sexual harassment?	50%	50%
Has your organization taken any action to promote gender equity?	73%	27%
Have you ever experienced a personal victory over gender bias in your profession?	38%	62%
Have you ever experienced a professional advantage due to being a woman?	57%	43%
Do you foresee any barriers to reaching your career goals?	64%	36%

			Yes	No
Have you ever had a mentor?			70%	30%

If yes, was your mentor:	Formal/ Assigned	Informal		
	15%	85%		

	Female	Male		
	34%	66%		

	Very	Some- what	Not at All
How prevalent is gender discrimination for women in your organization?	18%	65%	17%
How supportive is your organization in meeting the needs of working mothers?	24%	60%	16%

[a]Percentages are rounded to the nearest 1. Totals may vary between 99 and 101 due to rounding the percentages.

[b]For the purpose of this study, gender inequity is defined as differential or exclusionary treatment in the workplace based solely on gender.

Notes

CHAPTER ONE

1. Joan E. Rigdon, "Three Decades After the Equal Pay Act, Women's Wages Remain Far From Parity, *Wall Street Journal*, 6 July 1993, p. B1.
2. Ibid.
3. California Commission on the Status of Women, *A Profile of California Women: Employment*, May 19, 1993, p. 14.
4. Rochelle Sharpe, "Women Make Strides, But Men Stay Firmly in Top Company Jobs," *Wall Street Journal*, 29 March 1994, p. A10.
5. "A Half-Milestone for Corporate Boards, *Business Week*, November 21, 1994, 6.
6. Fred Danzig and Melanie Wells, "'Old Boys' Network' Still Alive," *Advertising Age*, May 24, 1993, 40.
7. Sue Shellenbarger, "Work-Force Study Finds Loyalty Is Weak, Divisions of Race and Gender Are Deep," *Wall Street Journal*, September 3, 1993, pp. B1, B8.
8. Betsy Morris, "Executive Women Confront Midlife Crisis," *Fortune*, September 18, 1995, 68.
9. Julia Lawlor, "Executive Exodus," *Working Woman*, November 1994, 40.
10. The Federal Glass Ceiling Commission, *Good for Business: Making Full Use of the Nation's Capital*, March 1995, p. 10.
11. Lisa Mainiero, "The Longest Climb," *Psychology Today*, November/December 1994, 40–43.
12. Sharpe, "Women Make Strides, But Men Stay Firmly in Top Company Jobs," A10.

CHAPTER TWO

1. Kathleen Koman, "Catalytic Chemist," *Harvard Magazine*, January/February 1995, 52.

CHAPTER THREE

1. Korn/Ferry International and UCLA Anderson Graduate School of Management, *Decade of the Executive Woman*, 1993, 15.

2. Margaret Hennig and Anne Jardim, *The Managerial Woman*, New York: Pocket Books, 1978, 47.

3. Sylvia Senter, *Women at Work*, New York: Coward, McCann, and Geohegan, 1982, 155.

CHAPTER FOUR

1. Harris Collingwood, "Women As Managers: Not Just Different — Better," *Working Woman*, November 1995, 14.

2. "Affirmative Action," *Working Woman*, October 1995, 90.

3. Editorial, "Excuse Me, Are Women Equal Yet?" *Glamour*, February 1996, 91.

4. Ibid.

5. Taylor Cox Jr. and Carol Smolinski, "Managing Diversity and Glass Ceiling Initiatives As National Economic Imperatives," U.S. Department of Labor, January 31, 1994, 18-19.

6. Cynthia Fuchs Epstein, *Glass Ceilings and Open Doors: Women's Advancement in the Legal Profession*, Report to the Committee on Women in the Profession, Association of the Bar of the City of New York, 1995, 85.

7. "White, Male, and Worried," *Business Week*, January 31, 1994, 52.

8. Cynthia Fuchs Epstein, *Glass Ceilings and Open Doors*, 34.

CHAPTER FIVE

1. The Federal Glass Ceiling Commission, *Good for Business: Making Full Use of the Nation's Capital*, 9, 11.

2. "A Half-Milestone for Corporate Boards, *Business Week*, November 21, 1994, 6.

3. Judith Waldrop, "The Demographics of Decision Makers," *American Demographics*, June 1993, p. 28.

4. Editorial, "Excuse Me, Are Women Equal Yet?" 91.

5. Korn/Ferry International and UCLA Anderson Graduate School of Management, *Decade of the Executive Woman*, 15.

6. James M. Kouzes and Barry Z. Posner, *The Leadership Challenge* (San Francisco: Jossey-Bass, 1987), 77.

7. Hennig and Jardim, *The Managerial Woman*, 13.

8. Ibid., 13-14.

CHAPTER SIX

1. Andrea Sachs, "9-Zip! I Love It!" *Time*, November 22, 1993, 45.

2. Korn/Ferry International and UCLA Anderson Graduate School of Management, *Decade of the Executive Woman*, 34.
3. Mary P. Rowe, "People Who Feel Harassed Need a Complaint System with Both Formal and Informal Options," *Negotiation Journal*, April 1990, 164.
4. Ibid., 161.
5. Massachusetts Institute of Technology, *Dealing with Harassment at MIT* (Cambridge, Mass.: Massachusetts Institute of Technology, 1993), 29.

CHAPTER EIGHT

1. Donna Brown Hogarty, "Careerwise," *New Woman*, September 1994, 52.
2. Diane E. Lewis, "Anxiously Expecting," *The Boston Globe*, 16 July 1995, p. 79.
3. Deborah K. Holmes and Dana E. Friedman, *The Changing Employer-Employee Contract: The Role of Work-Family Issues* (New York: Families and Work Institute, 1995), 2.

CHAPTER NINE

1. Edie Fraser, "Women & Networking," *Working Women*, November 1995, 69.
2. U. S. Department of Labor, Women's Bureau, *Women Workers: Trends and Issues* (1993), 250.
3. CS First Boston, "Update on the Women's Task Force," April 19, 1994, 1.
4. Ibid., 7.
5. Brown, Rudnick, Freed and Gesmer, "A History of the Women's Rountable," 1995, 1.
6. Lawlor, "Executive Exodus," 40.
7. Women in Development of Greater Boston, *Getting What You Deserve: A Reference Guide to Compensation and Salary Negotiation* (1992), p. i.
8. Harvard-Smithsonian Center for Astrophysics, Space for Women: Perspectives on Careers in Science (1994), 9.
9. Ibid., 9, 12.

CHAPTER TEN

1. Mary Rowe, "Building 'Mentoring' Frameworks for Women (and Men) as Part of an Effective Equal Opportunity Ecology," in *Sex Discrimination in Higher Education: Strategies for Equality*, ed. Jennie Farley (Ithaca, N.Y.: Cornell University Press, 1981), appendix, 1, 4.

2. Deborah Tannen, *Talking from 9 to 5* (New York: William Morrow, 1994), 136.
3. Ibid., 157.
4. Hal Lancaster, "Two Women Hire Help to Smash the Glass Ceiling," *Wall Street Journal*, 14 November 1995, p. B1.
5. Rowe, "Building 'Mentoring' Frameworks for Women (and Men)," appendix, 1, 4.

Chapter Eleven

1. Lawlor, "Executive Exodus," 40.
2. Catalyst, news release, "Catalyst Surveys Senior Women Executives and CEOs on Women's Progress in Corporate Leadership," February 27, 1996, 1.
3. Ibid., 1–2.
4. Walecia Konrad, "Welcome to the Women-Friendly Company," *Business Week*, August 6, 1990, 54.
5. Ann B. Morris, Randall P. White, Ellen Van Velsor, and the Center for Creative Leadership, *Breaking the Glass Ceiling* (Reading, Mass.: Addison-Wesley, 1987.)
6. Catalyst, "Catalyst Surveys Senior Women," 5.
7. Cynthia Fuchs Epstein, *Glass Ceilings and Open Doors*, 49.
8. Morris, "Executive Women Confront Midlife Crisis," 68.
9. The Conference Board, "Work-Family Roundtable: The Glass Ceiling," (summer 1995), 4.
10. Denise Allen Zwicker, "SCH Begins to Break the Glass Ceiling," Intermission.
11. Shari Caudron, "Sexual Politics," *Personnel Journal*, May 1995, 52.

Chapter Twelve

1. Quality Connection, "The Glass Ceiling in Health Care: A Roundtable Discussion," (fall 1995), 3.
2. "White, Male, and Worried," 52.

INDEX